P9-DIG-907

KOREAN
Etiquette & Ethics
in
Business

KOREAN

Etiquette & Ethics
in
Business

WITHDRAWN

Theodore Lownik Library
Illinois Benedictine College
Lisle, Illinois 60532

Boye De Mente

NTC Business Books
a division of National Textbook Company • Lincolnwood Illinois U.S.A.

HF
5387
.D385
1988

Published by NTC Business Books, Trade Imprint of National Textbook Company,
4255 West Touhy Avenue, Lincolnwood (Chicago), Illinois 60646-1975 U.S.A.
Copyright © 1988 by Boye De Mente. All rights reserved. No part of this book may be reproduced,
stored in a retrieval system, or transmitted in any form, or by any means, electronic, mechanical,
photocopying or otherwise, without the prior written permission of National Textbook Company.
Manufactured in the United States of America.
Library of Congress Catalog Card Number: 87-62403

8 9 0 ML 9 8 7 6 5 4 3 2

Contents

Introduction
The "Force" Is with Them

Out-Japanizing Japan

The Republic of South Korea (ROK), a tiny nation of thirty-five million people perched precariously on the southern half of the Korean Peninsula, is one of the great success stories of the century.

When the ancient kingdom of Korea was freed from Japanese colonial rule at the end of World War II in 1945, the country was an economic wasteland. Things were then made much worse by the division of the peninsula into two separate countries—Soviet-dominated Communist North Korea, and American-dominated South Korea.

In 1950, just five years later, the North Korean army, backed by Russia and China, unleashed a blitzkrieg attack against South Korea in an attempt to bring the entire peninsula under communist rule. The invading North Korean and Chinese armies were finally repulsed by a combined force of American, South Korean, and United Nations troops, but not before much of the Republic of South Korea had once again been ravaged by the insanity of war.

Following an armistice in 1953, the people of South Korea once more began the seemingly insurmountable task of rebuilding their country. But they were plagued by an inefficient, corrupt government, a feudalistic society, lack of an industrial base, and an untrained labor force, and progress was painfully slow.

It was not until 1962 that a new government established the framework for an economic development program that was to propel South Korea, with startling speed, into the ranks of the world's leading economic powers—and in actuality, achieve a far greater miracle than the Japanese had accomplished.

While there were many external factors that contributed to the miracle of South Korea—with almost total access to the affluent American market being foremost—the basic grounds for the Phoenix-like transformation of the minuscule country into an economic powerhouse were internal, and consisted primarily of the special character, ambitions, and energy of the people.

Releasing the Power of *Hahn*

There is a word in the Korean language that expresses a condition and a concept that I have often used in discussing Mexicans and other people with long histories of being oppressed and emotionally, intellectually, and physically abused. This Korean word is *hahn,* and it is used in reference to the psychic force that is now driving Koreans to perform almost superhuman feats in overcoming the terrible legacy of their past.

As far as I know, there is no similar word in any other language, and if it should turn out to be unique to Korea, it is a word that all should learn because it could play a vital role in others' achieving a better understanding of human needs and aspirations, and consequently lead to a better concept of social and political systems.

Hahn cannot be defined in one or two words or even several words, but it has a very clear, exact meaning. It refers to the buildup of unrequited yearnings that are brought about by oppressive religious and political systems; by living in a society in which most of the normal human drives are subverted or totally denied; by living in a state of constant fear; and by intense and permanent feelings of frustration, repressed anger, regret, remorse, grief, deprivation, and inability to change things.

Korean social and medical authorities identify many kinds of *hahn* that have played key roles in molding Korean character: the *hahn* of poverty, the *hahn* of status immobility, the *hahn* of sex discrimination, the *hahn* of political abuse, the *hahn* of colonialism and suffering caused by war, the *hahn* of educational deprivation, the *hahn* of political strife and stifled ambitions—all the institutionalized limitations on human freedom and all the hardships the people have been forced to endure over the ages.

For centuries, political and religious leaders kept the people of Korea under a giant lid that prevented them from developing even the smallest fraction of their potential. They became like steel springs pressed nearly flat, with no way to release their energy, curiosity, or creativity.

All this repressed energy, all the repressed needs and aspirations of the Koreans over some five thousand years, is what makes up the psychic force that now motivates and energizes them, and is bringing about a miraculous transformation of the Korean economy and society as a whole.

It is this released energy of *hahn* that today drives Koreans to get an education, to work with a kind of frenzy, to be adaptable, disciplined, and tenacious; to sacrifice themselves for the betterment of their families and their country.

The Korean way of doing business is, of course, a natural outgrowth of its five-thousand-year history, and to successfully engage in business with Korea requires substantial knowledge of the unique social and corporate culture that has evolved from this history.

In this book, I have tried to provide the cultural background and insights that are essential to this understanding and to the development of practical, mutually beneficial relations with Korea.

Boye De Mente
Seoul, Korea

I

Meeting with Korea

Life on a High-Tension Wire

The appeal of Korea—its people and culture—can be so powerful that it virtually mesmerizes Westerners, or it can have the opposite effect and turn them off completely.

In the words of Carole Alexander, formerly director of public relations for the Westin Chosun Hotel in Seoul: "There are so many things, good and bad, that are so different, so unexpected, that life here is far more intense than back home. There are little things that 'jerk your wire' every day."

She added: "Most Koreans try so hard to please, to accommodate. Americans in particular are looked on as a little larger than life."

Another Korean characteristic that Alexander singled out as a positive factor is their innate honesty. "It is fearsome," she said. "A taxi driver will hunt for hours to find a passenger who left money in his cab. Restaurant employees will go to extremes to return forgotten parcels and other items. The basic honesty of the average Korean is startling in today's cynical world."

Vendors often leave wares on the sidewalks overnight, covering them with a plastic or canvas sheet—to keep the dust and possibly insects off them rather than to deter thieves.

Personal safety is also seen as one of the attractions of expatriate living in Korea. There is virtually no danger of personal violence against foreign visitors or residents. Violent crimes outside of family situations are rare. Vandalism is almost nonexistent, as is graffiti.

Koreans are not only especially well mannered, with a stern etiquette code, they are also acutely concerned about their appearance. They are especially clothes-conscious, having been culturally conditioned for centuries to recognize and respect uniforms and the official apparel of various social classes. The average Korean businessman dresses well so consistently that there is a standing joke that all Korean males are born in three-piece suits.

Areas of Seoul and other larger Korean cities are completely Westernized and ultramodern. Many shopping areas would not be out of place on Beverly Hills' Rodeo Drive. Koreans are proud of this progress and like to show it off. Among the most conspicuous symbols of the rapid progress Korea has made are its hotels. Seoul now boasts several world-class luxury hotels that provide a quality of food and service that is unsurpassed. Businessmen who are veteran Seoul visitors often prefer the Westin Chosun because of its central location, business offices (including the American Chamber of Commerce in Korea), and its Western flavor, but many of the city's other hotels, including Hotel Shilla, Hotel Lotte, the Seoul Hilton International, and the Hyatt Regency Seoul, are on a par with the great hotels of Tokyo, Hong Kong, Singapore, and Bangkok.

Conspicuous consumption by affluent businessmen, doctors, entertainers, and lawyers is common but still relatively discreet in Seoul. Large apartments and homes, some with swimming pools, membership in exclusive golf clubs, sumptuous wedding parties at the luxury-class international hotels, and "fraternal debauches" at upscale hostess bars have become the prerogatives of Korea's new rich.

One of the most conspicuous signs of affluence is the size and location of one's home or apartment. Anything over sixty *pyong* (3.3 square meters per *pyong*), especially if it is on a plot larger than one hundred *pyong*, puts one in the category of the well-to-do.

Memberships in exclusive golf clubs and health clubs, although still regarded primarily as a business expense, have also become a separate sign of social status. Among the highest ranked clubs in the country are the Seoul Country Club, the Hanyang Country Club, and the invitation-only Anyang Country Club, owned by the Samsung Group. Those who have really arrived often have member ships in more than one club.

The Danger of False Impressions

The first-time visitor to Korea, no matter how well educated or experienced in other fields, typically makes a number of value judgments about the people and the country that are partially or totally wrong. Because the people and the cities have a contemporary Western look, the uninitiated visitor all too often falls into the trap of automatically presuming that the character, personality, and proclivities of the Koreans themselves have also been Westernized.

While this is true in part for a few thousand people who were educated abroad, well over ninety percent of all Koreans still reflect the traditions and conditioning of over a thousand years of Shamanism, Confucianism, and Buddhism—with Confucianism being the paramount influence in the culture for the last five hundred years. The attitudes and actions of most Koreans can be understood only in Confucian terms. Any effective relationship with them must be solidly founded on Confucian precepts.

This situation is easy to describe, and the forewarned newcomer may readily accept it intellectually. But accepting it emotionally and incorporating it into one's thoughts and actions on a daily, practical basis is extremely difficult, and usually happens only over a relatively long period of personal experience. Advance knowledge will substantially shorten this learning process, however, and help one avoid serious mistakes in the interim.

The Violence Factor

While virtually all Koreans, particularly those born before 1950, are imbued with the traditional Confucian principles of strict order and obedience to authority, they are also influenced by a growing concept of political democracy mixed with strong nationalistic feelings and a tendency toward extremely emotional, violent actions in support of their beliefs.

These strongly nationalistic feelings and raw emotionalism, fed by a long memory of foreign domination and exploitation, make Koreans especially sensitive to criticism or pressure to reform or internationalize their legal and economic system. Korean news media have exacerbated this situation in the past by strident attacks against the U.S., which has spoken out against Korea's discriminatory and self-serving practices.

Korean students in particular have responded by attacking U.S. government facilities in Pusan and other Korean cities. Obviously both American and Korean leaders (and news media) must achieve a better understanding of the volatile nature of their differences, and bring these differences to the negotiating table instead of the streets.

As with understanding any people, the first step is a good grasp of their history.

2

The Making of Korea

The Early Kingdoms

The Korean Peninsula has been inhabited for at least thirty thousand years, and perhaps for tens of thousands of years longer. Prior to 1000 B.C. family clans lived in villages, tilled the fields around them, hunted, and fished. Their religion consisted of Shamanism, in which natural objects such as trees, rivers, and rocks were believed to have spirits. (The same religion survives today, especially in rural areas.)

Korea's Bronze Age began around 1000 B.C., lasted for about a thousand years, and was followed by an Iron Age, which ended in approximately A.D. 935. In 350 B.C. the first tribal league, Chosun, centered in north Korea, was at the apex of its power. Other tribal groups that existed at that time included Chinhan, Pyonhan, and Mahan.

During the next three hundred years, these tribal leagues evolved into a number of competing kingdoms—Silla (57 B.C. to A.D. 935), Paekche (18 B.C. to A.D. 600), and Koguryo (37 B.C. to A.D. 668).

Heavily influenced by China, their huge neighbor, which was centuries ahead of them in cultural achievements, the people of the various kingdoms of Korea had developed a sophisticated lifestyle by the first century A.D., including the invention of a central radiant heating system for their homes that was known as *ondol*, and is still in use in most of Korea today.

Cultural development continued at a rapid pace during the next several centuries, with Buddhism and Confucianism being added to the native religion of Shamanism. Society became divided into classes patterned after the system in China, with the royal family and elite government administrators and educators at the top. Those wishing to enter governmental service competed in annual examinations.

In A.D. 668 the kingdom of Silla became supreme throughout the peninsula, and gave Korea its first golden age. When Silla was at its peak, between A.D. 700 and 800, the capital city of Kyongju had a population of over one million, and was one of the most modern cities in the world. Many of Korea's greatest Buddhist temples were built during this period. This was also the period that saw the rise of unarmed martial arts.

The Silla dynasty gave way to the Koryo dynasty (from which modern Korea takes its name) in A.D. 935. The Koryo king gave Buddhism special status in the country in A.D. 950, resulting in its playing a dominant role in the history of the country until the fall of the dynasty in 1392. Confucianism, which is more of a social system than a religion, also permeated Korean culture during the Koryo period, and was to have its heyday during the next great dynasty.

The importance of Buddhism and Confucianism, both of which relied on written texts for their propagation, led to Korea's first printing press, which originally used wooden blocks and then began using movable metal type in A.D. 1234. Korea's famed celadon pottery was also developed during this period.

In the latter part of the 1200s, Genghis Khan and his Mongol hordes made Koryo a vassal state of China. King Kojong fled to the island of Kwangha, where he had all the Buddhist scriptures carved on 81,258 wooden blocks, an undertaking that required sixteen years. (The blocks may be seen today at the Haein-Sa Mountain Temple.) The Mongol influence in Korea lasted for over one hundred years.

The Last Dynasty

Korea's last great dynasty was founded in A.D. 1392, when General Song-Gye Yi seized power. Yi moved the capital to Seoul, its present location. The general's descendants were to rule Korea until 1910, when the entire peninsula was annexed by Japan.

The greatest of the Yi kings was Sejong, who ascended the throne in 1418. An enlightened and progressive ruler, Sejong established schools throughout the country, where learned professors taught political science, history, medicine, geography, and other subjects, including Confucianism. Sejong is personally credited with making significant technological advances in water clocks, the sundial, rain gauges, and the lunar calendar. He was also responsible for setting up a team of scholars to specifically devise a purely Korean system of writing, called *hangul* (hahn-guul), for the country's language.

Contact with Japan

Up to this period, Korea's relations with Japan had mostly been friendly. In fact, Korea, along with China, had been the wellspring for much of Japanese civilization. But in the mid-1400s, Japanese pirates began raiding the Korean coastal areas, and thereafter relations between the two countries deteriorated.

Confucianism gradually became the primary foundation of the Korean culture. In 1471 the principles of Confucianism were codified in the Great Administration Code and made the law of the land. The law officially established four distinct hereditary social classes—the *yangban*, made up of scholars (*moonban*) and military officers (*muban*) at the top; the *joong-in*, made up of professionals (doctors, lawyers, geographers, translators, and middle-ranked military officers); the *sang-min*, which included artisans, craftsmen, fishermen, farmers who were ex-soldiers, and merchants. The lowest class was made up of servants, butchers, entertainers, *kisaeng* girls, sorcerers, felons, and slaves.

The code also decreed that only direct lineal male members of the highest class (the *yangban*) were eligible to take the civil service examinations for government service, which had been held annually since the year A.D. 655.

Part of the preparation for the civil service exams was learning some twenty thousand Chinese characters (King Sejong's simplified *hangul* characters didn't count), and mastering the art of calligraphy.

During the more than five hundred years of the Yi dynasty, several generations usually lived in a family compound—the men in the front and the women in the back. Boys and girls were separated at the age of seven, at which time boys started school while girls were kept at home and in lower-class families acted as servants to the male members of the family. When sons married, they set up housekeeping in their family compound.

Men were free to come and go as they pleased, but women were virtually slaves. Upper-class women were prohibited from leaving their compounds during the day, and could go out at night for brief periods only with the permission of their husbands. In Seoul, the hour at which the women could leave their homes and go outside was noted by the ringing of a great bell, which also sounded when they were to be back in their homes. Because of this strictly enforced edict, many women lived all their lives without seeing Seoul during daylight hours.

Men could divorce their wives at any time for any one of seven "sins," among which were talking too much, not pleasing their mothers-in-law, and failure to bear sons.

This social system prevailed in Korea until well into the twentieth century, and was responsible for fashioning what is now often referred to as the traditional Korean character.

The Coming of the Japanese

In 1592, Japan's Hideyoshi Toyotomi, who had just recently become the supreme military power in Japan after a long period of clan warfare, sent a huge army to Korea, determined to conquer the peninsula and then proceed on to invade China—apparently to extract revenge from the Chinese for the attempted invasions of Japan by Genghis

Khan and his Mongol hordes in 1274 and 1281. However, the first Japanese invasion ships to approach Korea were defeated by Korea's famed Admiral Sun-Shin Yi, whose ironclad warships, the world's first, caught the Japanese by surprise.

But the large Japanese army of skilled and experienced warriors was not to be denied. They eventually established a beachhead, then began a systematic campaign of laying waste to the country and butchering everyone who opposed them.

The Japanese troops occupied large portions of Korea and settled in for a long campaign. Among those joining the Japanese occupying forces was a Spanish Catholic priest, who began preaching Christianity to Koreans in the conquered areas. He was the first Westerner of record to set foot in Korea. Before the Japanese army could complete the subjugation of Korea, however, Hideyoshi Toyotomi became ill. Fearful that his newly established military control of Japan might be threatened, he had the army recalled from Korea. He died before they could reach Japan and prevent his fears from coming true.

The death and destruction wrought on Korea by the Japanese soured Koreans on having any kind of foreign relations. The country was sealed off to the outside world and was to be known as "The Hermit Kingdom" for almost three hundred years.

Ironically, it was also to be Japan that pried the Hermit Kingdom open, then brought its downfall. In 1876, a Japanese ship appeared off the coast of southern Korean, and was fired on by shore batteries. When the ship's crew reported the incident, the highly militant Japanese mounted a crushing attack against the inexperienced and primitively armed Korean defense forces, and once again established a beachhead on Korean soil.

Colonialization by Japan

Japan demanded that Korea renounce its isolationist policy and open its ports to Japanese naval and merchant ships (in an almost exact reenactment of their own experiences—

minus the invasion—with the United States in the 1850s). Six years later, Korea extended the same rights to the U.S., and shortly thereafter to other nations as well.

From this time on, Japan rapidly extended its influence in Korea, resulting in a breakdown of its relations with China and Russia. Following its successful war against China in 1895 and against Russia in 1904–1905, Japan began the all-out colonialization of Korea, taking over the government and all major industries. In 1910 Japan made Korea a part of the Japanese empire, and began a brutal program aimed at Japanizing the Koreans by outlawing their language and many of their cultural practices, and forcing them to follow Japanese customs.

Japanese control of Korea continued until 1945, when Japan was defeated by the U.S. and Allied Powers. Unfortunately, the U.S. agreed to allow Russia to administer the portion of Korea north of the 38th parallel until a Korean government could be established to replace the defeated Japanese. The Russians immediately established a communist regime in northern Korea, refusing all entreaties to reunite the country.

Elections were held in South Korea in 1948. Syngman Rhee was elected president. In the meantime, Il-Sung Kim, a dedicated communist, was installed as president of North Korea.

In June 1950, after five years of communist indoctrination, North Korean troops invaded South Korea, believing that the only way to reunite their country was to drive the Americans out of South Korea.

U.S. and United Nations troops pushed the invading North Koreans back to the Yalu River, and the war seemed to be over. China then joined the fighting on the side of North Korea. American and UN forces suffered heavy losses and were driven southward to the vicinity of Seoul.

General Douglas MacArthur, Supreme Commander of the Allied Powers occupying Japan at that time, led the American forces in a counterattack through Inchon that outflanked the Chinese and North Koreans and drove them back to the 38th parallel, where the war became stalemated. A cease-fire was called and in July 1953 an armistice agreement was signed, establishing a two-kilometer demilitarized zone along the 38th parallel and setting up the framework for peace talks between the North and South.

The talks are still going on, and the country is still divided. Families that were torn apart have not seen each other since 1950. And like the Communist Wall in Berlin, the demilitarized zone and the peace-talk site at Panmunjom have become tourist attractions.

The Ordeal Continues

The three-year war brought new death and destruction to the Koreans. But the suffering of the Korean people was not over. The government under Syngman Rhee was rife with corruption and the abuse of power. Student uprisings finally forced Rhee to retire in 1960. The government was run for a short period by President Myun J. Chang. In May 1961 he was toppled by General Chung-Hee Pak in a bloodless coup.

For the next eight years Pak gave South Korea harsh but efficient rule, instituting many reforms and inaugurating the first of a series of five-year plans that were to create an economic miracle. Pak was assassinated in October 1979. Kyu-Hah Choi served as president for two months, and was replaced on December 12, 1979, by Doo-Hwan Chun, under whose strict military-style leadership the economic miracle of the Republic of South Korea continued to unfold.

In early 1987, disenchantment with the militaristic regime of ex-General Doo-Hwan Chun reached a boiling point. University students once again took to the streets, bringing on a series of increasingly violent confrontations with the national police and armed forces.

Finally, Tae-Woo Roh, newly appointed chairman of the ruling Democratic Justice Party and Chun's hand-picked successor, abruptly capitulated to the demands of the students and the main opposition parties, announcing in late June that the constitution would be revised and a democratic form of government adopted.

It is against this backdrop of Shamanism, Buddhism, Confucianism, a strict hierarchal society, and decades of suffering and anguish at the hands of foreign powers and internal political strife that one must view present-day South Korea and its people.

3

Defining the Korean Way

Korea *vs.* Japan

In almost any reference to how business is done in Korea, there is a strong tendency to make comparisons with Japan. There are indeed many similarities between the social and business customs in the two countries. In fact, the primary cultural components of the two countries spring from the same roots, and the most significant difference between the two is that in Korea these cultural components are much stronger than they are in Japan.

However, Koreans do not like Korea to be regarded as a "second Japan," or for themselves to be thought of as imitating the Japanese. They are quick to point out that virtually all the main themes and threads of "Japanese culture" came from Korea, or from China through Korea. They go beyond this, in fact, pointing to substantial evidence which clearly indicates that the first central kingdom of Japan was founded by Korean tribesmen whose leader was the first emperor of Japan, and whose direct descendant today sits on the throne of Japan. Some say that the Japanese language is a derivative of Korean.

Because of random historical events, Japan was opened to Western influence much earlier than Korea, first in the 1500s and then totally in the 1850s, while Korea's feudal history and isolation from the rest of the world did not end until 1945. Japan thus has had more than a hundred years' start on Korea in industrializing its economy and interacting with the rest of the world community.

The history of "modern" Korea actually did not begin until the end of the Korean War in 1953, and during the brief span of time since then, Korea has accomplished much more of an economic miracle than that which occurred in post–World War II Japan. Starting out with a much smaller land base, a much smaller population, a primitive education system, an unskilled labor force, virtually no one in government or business with international experience, no hidden assets (such as existed in Japan), with far less economic assistance from the U.S. than Japan received, plus other handicaps ranging from a constant security threat to a harsher climate and remote geographic location, Korea, by an astounding display of courage, unstinted ambition, perseverance, and hard work, became a world-class economic power in less than thirty years.

In many ways, Korea today is where Japan was in the 1890s in terms of distance from its feudal past. Yet it is now less than twenty years behind Japan in economic progress, and is ahead of Japan in some crucial areas of internationalization, particularly in developing an intensely dedicated cadre of bilingual, bicultural managers, and in employing and making full use of Western-educated technicians, engineers, and scientists.

While much more traditional in a cultural sense than the Japanese, Koreans are much less hidebound by cultural restraints in interfacing with Westerners. The Japanese readily admit to being uncomfortable in the presence of Westerners. Older generations are very frank in saying they prefer not to associate or work with Westerners at all, and in moments of exceptional candor, admit to disliking Westerners.

Koreans are much more relaxed and natural in their relationships with Westerners. They are much more direct in their likes and dislikes, and are therefore also easier for Westerners to understand.

Despite strong Korean objections to being compared with the Japanese, it is obvious that previous Japan experience is beneficial to the foreigner doing business in Korea. Marvin J. Winship, formerly Director of Operations in Korea for International Executive Service Corps, said his early experiences in Japan had been invaluable in coming to terms with the business environment in Korea. He added: "I have been coming to Korea on business since 1958, and over the years have had hundreds of conversations about Korean etiquette and ethics in business. The biggest challenge now, it seems to me, is to keep up with the changes, to distinguish between what is still traditional Korean and what has been grafted onto the Korean system from the U.S. or other Western countries. I often need help in understanding the degree of these changes."

Internationalization

The "internationalization" of Korea is proceeding rapidly, much faster it seems than it is in Japan. Among other things, Koreans do not feel compelled (as the Japanese do) to Koreanize everything that comes into the country. One good example of this is the treatment of foreign words that are adopted into the languages. In Japan foreign words are Japanized and pronounced as if they were Japanese—with the result that it is often extremely difficult, and sometimes impossible, for foreign students of Japanese to divine the meaning of the formerly English terms. An example: *sabai-buru*, which is "survival" pronounced in Japanese. Unless read or heard in very clear and specific context, "sabai-buru" is meaningless to the native English speaker.

Rather than go this route, the Korean Ministry of Education (in 1985) adopted a system of writing foreign words in the Korean alphabet that maintains as far as possible the original pronunciation. In the coming years this will make a significant contribution to the ability of Koreans and English-speaking people to communicate with each other.

Korean Conduct

The basic conduct and character of Koreans is founded in the principles and teachings of Confucianism, which permeated the culture of the country socially and politically from 1392 to 1910—more than five hundred years. The primary precepts of Confucianism were:

1. Total loyalty to a hierarchal structure of authority—the parents, family, clan, community, and king or nation.

2. Duty to the parents, incorporating loyalty, love, and gratitude, especially to the mother, who was portrayed (and usually was) a symbol of virtue, unselfishness, and sacrifice.

3. Strict order and a minutely defined form of conduct between children and adults, with children conditioned to pay absolute respect to their grandparents and parents, in that order, to obey them totally, and to demonstrate only the most respectful behavior toward them, including the use of respect language, bowing, and speaking only when spoken to. This extreme conditioning explains, of course, the respect present-day Koreans still have for older people, teachers, and government officials.

No doubt in compensation for these strict rules of etiquette and conduct demanded of all young people in Korea, the very young were allowed to run free, almost without any discipline in the rest of their behavior, until they were about ten years old.

4. Separation of the husband and wife. Men and women in Confucian Korea lived almost totally in separate spheres. Men lived in the front of the compound; their wives in the back. Men concerned themselves with outside affairs and the overall running of the family compound; women performed all of the housekeeping functions and the raising of the children, with absolutely no crossing over. Boys were sent to school to learn to read and write; girls were taught domestic skills at home.

5. Trust between friends was upheld as a prime virtue, and was strongly emphasized as a vital part of the overall fabric of the society on a community level.

While the Confucian culture of early Korea was responsible for one of the most peaceful and orderly societies that ever existed, there was also a downside to its extreme curtailment of the natural curiosity, creativity, and individuality of human beings.

Both Korean and foreign observers, commenting on Korea's Confucian society in the early part of the twentieth century, noted that the narrow constrictions of the social system, suppressing as it did many of the natural impulses of the people, resulted in their being extremely emotional and hot-tempered, and inclined toward outbursts of rage, jealousy, cruelty, and violence.

One story has it that to help prevent fights among men, King Sejong in the early 1400s decreed that all men would wear heavy hats made of pottery, with severe penalties for anyone who allowed his hat to fall off or be knocked off. Some decades later it became the custom to make these large hats of horsehair instead of clay. (I suspect that this is where the old saying, "He would fight at the drop of a hat," came from.)

The social, political, and educational systems in feudal Korea also negated the development of abstract, metaphysical, and rational reasoning, which in turn resulted in irrational behavior when the people were confronted with any situation outside of their highly structured lifestyle. The Confucian teachings and lifestyle also prevented the development of a separate sense of responsibility and ability to self-reflect on moral issues.

Dr. Kyong-Dong Kim, Professor and Director, Social Science Institute, Seoul National University, has come up with a long list of cultural characteristics of the Koreans that might be categorized as the "isms of Korea." These include:

Authoritarianism—Emphasizing a superior-subordinate relationship between parents and children, the old and the young, male and female, and upper and lower social classes and ranks.

Collectivism—A strong inclination to look at everything and react to everything in terms of "familism," with the accompanying inability to quickly and easily distinguish between what is private and what is public.

Connectionism—The deeply rooted habit of establishing all social and business relationships on personal connections (instead of more abstract factors such as mutual interests or mutual activities).

Conservatism—A continuing belief in the value of traditional ways and a tendency to be traditional in behavior.

Exclusivism—A strong tendency to form exclusive groups or factions centered on personal relations, such as family, school, birthplace, and community, which leads in turn to favoritism and nepotism.

Fatalism—Acceptance of things they think cannot be changed, such as abuse by politicians or browbeating by superiors, which leads to submissiveness and feelings of inferiority to outside authorities or power.

Secularism—A strong emphasis on worldly accomplishments, on working harder than anyone else, on producing more than anyone else, on building things bigger and better than anyone else.

The Changing Korean Character

Korea today is nothing at all like it was in the 1950s or 1960s or even 1970s, and yet it has changed very little in the underlying principles of society and business. Liberation from Japanese rule in 1945 and from American dominance in the 1950s was followed by the rapid introduction of a Western façade that has changed the appearance of its cities and to a lesser degree its countryside. But this image of scientific industrialism is, for the most part, only on the surface.

Thousands of Koreans have been ostensibly de-Koreanized by years of exposure to and involvement with Westerners, particularly Americans, and other thousands have been educated abroad and are now either bicultural or at least bilingual and able to function in both a Korean and an

American environment. But generally speaking they remain identifiably Korean in their basic attitudes and behavior.

The family is still of vital importance. There is still respect for authority, the aged, and the learned. All of the "isms" delineated by Dr. Kyong-Dong Kim are alive and well. It is impossible for a Korean or a Westerner to function effectively and efficiently in Korea without following the "Korean way" in many areas of life and work.

Dr. Kim says bluntly that Koreans are still emotional, relatively crude, superstitious, and aggressive—but not lazy—and that Korean society is still organized on an intricate network of personal connections; that it is still an authoritarian hierarchy; that people still resort to ritualistic face-saving façades, and emphasize class and rank.

But internal motivation for change, outside pressure for change, and the momentum of change are growing rapidly in Korea, and in fact will probably see Korea pull ahead of Japan in its rush to internationalize not only its economy but its society as well. Koreans are not as ethnocentric, not as antiforeign, not as arrogant, not as militaristic, not as determined as the Japanese to spread their way of doing things abroad.

This basic difference between Koreans and Japanese will be a major advantage to Korea in its future relations with the world at large.

Formal Etiquette Is Important

On the personal side, Koreans tend to be very formal in their meetings and receptions, particularly higher-ranking government officials and businessmen. Their treatment of Westerners also tends to be quite formal. They are especially respectful toward experienced businessmen and technical professionals, regarding them as teachers in the highest sense.

Like their Japanese neighbors and close kinsmen, the only time higher-ranking Korean businessmen and government officials dispense with formality is at Korean-style dinner parties, where there is a lot of eating, drinking, and interaction.

Learning How To Sing

The foreign businessman who really wants to make out in Korea will learn how to sing. That is a very big order for most Westerners, but it can be one of the most valuable skills you can have. Singing is an important part of the upbringing of Koreans, and is institutionalized at eating and drinking parties, where businessmen unwind, relax, enjoy themselves, and do the psychic communication that is so important to their emotions, spirit, mood—and image of other people.

Foreign businessmen are automatically expected to participate in these nighttime singing sessions, and not being able or willing to join in, no matter how badly one might perform, is a serious handicap. As silly as it might seem, any foreign businessman expecting to go to Korea should first lock himself in his bathroom (or go out in the desert, open fields, or mountains) and practice belting out two or three oldies that he is probably at least vaguely familiar with.

Being a really good singer is seen as a talent that is just as valuable as other desirable life skills—and sometimes more so, because it contributes directly to close communication and feelings of friendship and well-being.

The Personal Nature of Business

In Korea, as in many other Asian countries, business is a personal affair. The product, the profit, and everything else takes a backseat to personal relations. If you do not or cannot establish good personal relations with a large network of people, it is either difficult or impossible to do business in Korea. Personal relations and contacts, combined with a high sense of honor and trust, are the primary foundations of Korean business ethics. Written contracts are rare. Most business arrangements are based on verbal agreements.

As a result of this system, Koreans spend a significant amount of time expanding and nurturing their personal relations because their business depends on maintaining these relationships.

The foreign businessman wanting to succeed in Korea must adapt to this system to a substantial degree. It is essential that the foreign businessman program this kind of activity (and expenditure) into the time frame of his plans and expectations. The more you try to rush a decision or activity, particularly before the correct personal relationships have been established, the slower the process will be and the greater the likelihood that your efforts will fail.

"Many foreign businessmen believe that with the right product and price they can easily sell to or buy from any Korean company. This may be the case in Los Angeles or Hamburg but it doesn't always hold true in Korea," said Jon Saddoris, president of METEC, a business consulting firm in Seoul.

"Generally speaking, you are not going to get anywhere in Korea until you establish the necessary 'human relations,'" Saddoris adds. This includes approaching the company in the "correct manner," meaning through an acceptable introduction, and on the appropriate level.

Saddoris says that the first mistake many foreign businessmen make in their approach to doing business in Korea is to believe that meeting the president of a company and getting his approval and cooperation means smooth sailing from then on. In most cases, the managers—lower, middle, and upper—who actually run the company will resent being bypassed and will be less than cooperative, sometimes to the extent that the foreign proposal never gets off the ground floor.

If you have an introduction to the president, it is all right to meet him but you must also meet and establish a satisfactory relationship with the various managers, treating them with the same respect and concern that you extend to the president. This also applies to companies that are still in the hands of founders who appear to make all of the decisions.

In qualifying a Korean company it is essential that you determine the personal relationships between managers on all levels, especially the relationship between individual managers and directors or the president. Personal ties such as kinship, the same school, the same birthplace, or marriage often take precedence over job seniority, rank, or other factors, and may have a significant influence on who actually runs a company and how it is run. A clear understanding of these ties is often necessary to determine who the real decision-maker is in a Korean company.

Because human relations are so important in doing business with Korean companies, it is vital that you keep up to date on personnel and personal changes within any company concerned. The character and personality of a Korean company is as changeable as the ties and emotions of the people who make up the organization. It is therefore necessary to treat the relationship as a personal one, requiring regular stroking and other forms of maintenance.

Although Koreans now readily sign contracts with foreign companies, the contracts are invariably interpreted personally rather than in the legal sense, and are no better than the personal relationship that exists between the two parties. If the relationship is not constantly renewed and reinforced, the contract becomes just a piece of paper.

It is therefore very important for the foreign businessman going into business in Korea to be personally involved in the process of setting up the operation—along with obtaining the aid and advice of an experienced Korean to help him make his way through the intricate maze of connections and relationships that are involved.

Once an operation is established, the need for good, solid personal relations becomes more important, rather than diminishing. This means, of course, that the foreign side cannot sit back and relax as is so often the tendency. The Western habit of relying on contracts and lawyers does not work in the Korean environment.

Another aspect of the personal approach to business in Korea that often upsets Westerners is the tendency for

Koreans to run a company as an extended family, which means they make many decisions and take many actions that are based on purely personal factors instead of business considerations. The Westerner is not going to change this centuries old cultural characteristic, so the only recourse is to learn how to live with it.

The same personal approach necessary for the smooth functioning of an office or company also applies to a corporation's relations with government officials and bureaucrats. Most companies in Korea assign a particular individual to handle their government relations—invariably the senior member of the company who has the most experience in the bureaucratic arena, and "face" with key government officials.

Government bureaucrats in Korea are perhaps even more sensitive to the social and business status of people who approach them, and it is especially important for the foreign company having to deal with them to be aware of this. Sending in a young, low-status person is definitely not the way to go.

The Communication Problem

Since only a small percentage of Korean businessmen and government officials speak English, it is also important for the foreign businessman to learn some Korean, particularly if he is going to be in the country for several months or years. Just a small amount of ability in the language will go a long way in helping to make and sustain the kind of personal relations needed to function effectively—not necessarily in the conduct of business itself, but in greetings, casual comments, at eating and drinking parties, etc.

Language

Communication is, of course, a necessary foundation for understanding and cooperation, and while more and more Koreans are being educated abroad and becoming bilingual, and the number who learn English in local schools is also increasing rapidly, the foreign businessman who does not learn some Korean is greatly limited in both his professional and social contacts in Korea. Those who cannot communicate at all in Korean are severely handicapped in their ability to relate to and participate in life outside the narrow confines of the foreign community and world of international business.

Korean is generally described as difficult for English speakers to learn because it is unlike any Western language. Becoming really fluent in Korean is a formidable task, but learning enough of the language to communicate on a basic level is easy enough that anyone of average ability can accomplish this limited goal in two or three months of daily sustained study.

Korean is mostly made up of "pure Korean" and Chinese, along with a sizable number of words borrowed from Japanese and English. The Korean language is called *Hangugo* (hahn-guu-go) in Korean. The alphabet, created by a team of scholars in the 1400s at the behest of King Sejong, is called *Hangul* (hahn-guul). There are fourteen consonants and ten vowels in the language. Various combinations of these make up approximately fifty-four sounds or syllables. See the back of this book for a list of these syllables and a pronunciation chart.

Over the centuries very few Westerners ever learned Korean, resulting in their believing that the language was simply too difficult for foreigners to learn. As recently as the 1960s and early 1970s, Korean-speaking Westerners were so rare that most Koreans were amazed to encounter one who was able to speak the language—and they would often fail to understand the Korean-speaking foreigner because they simply couldn't conceive of that being possible. Anecdotes of Westerners speaking quite fluent Korean but getting only a blank stare in return were commonplace.

This situation has changed considerably since the 1970s. A significant percentage of the foreign businessmen stationed in Korea are students of the language and some of them speak it very well. Koreans in rural areas may still be surprised to hear Korean spoken by a foreigner, but this is no longer the case in the cities.

Because of the development of a superior-inferior social structure and a highly refined system of etiquette between and among classes of people, several different levels of language were also developed to distinguish between individuals and classes. The three most important basic levels of the language are an extraordinarily polite form used when addressing superiors, an intimate or familiar form for addressing close friends or equals, and a rough form used when speaking to people on a lower social level.

Becoming really fluent in Korean therefore means that one has to master these various levels, which is almost like learning three related but different languages. Fortunately, foreigners who are less than fluent are generally excused from this very strict social requirement and can get by with the use of familiar Korean in most situations. There are occasions, however, when the use of familiar speech is not appropriate and it is better either to speak in English or to remain silent.

As is often the case in the languages of Asia, there are a number of peculiarities in Korean and its use that must be quickly mastered by the foreigner who attempts to use the language on any level. It is very uncommon to use the single word *no* as a response, since just *no* is regarded as too abrupt, too impolite.

In Korean the appropriate response to a negative question is a negative—i.e., If you say "Don't you know his phone number?" The answer may be "Yes" (meaning yes, you are right. I don't know his phone number). This can cause both confusion and frustration, and can be avoided by phrasing all questions in the positive form.

If is one of the most commonly used words in the English language, but it is virtually untranslatable in Korean and gives a very negative image when used—because Koreans tend to associate its use with being uncertain and unable to make up one's mind.

The Great Divider

The one ethical area that probably causes Western businessmen more frustration than anything else in the Korean social system is the dichotomy between fairness and loyalty. To Westerners, particularly Americans, the bedrock of their ethical philosophy is fairness. This word is probably used more often than any other in our business discussions and negotiations.

In Korea, however, personal loyalty takes precedence over fairness.

When this difference in ethical codes is applied to business relationships, the results are very different, to say the least. It is therefore vital that the foreign businessman keep this distinctive Korean cultural value in mind at all times, and anticipate the effect it will have on everything he does in Korea, from dealing with government officials to haggling with a landlord over the cost of an apartment.

This is another area in which Western businessmen with limited cross-cultural experience typically make one error after another by either ignoring the fairness-loyalty factor altogether or playing it down because their inclination is to believe that everyone automatically understands and appreciates the concept of fairness, and will just as automatically accept it as the foundation for any business relationship.

The "Good Mood" Syndrome

Kibun (kee-boon), which means "feelings" or "mood," is one of the most important facets of Korean psychology. Koreans are extraordinarily sensitive to slights and setbacks which damage their *kibun* and upset the harmony of their existence, and they go to what appear to Westerners to be extreme lengths to maintain their own *kibun* as well as that of everyone else.

This conditioned cultural reflex influences virtually every nuance of the private as well as public lives of Koreans, and is part of their institutions of etiquette, politeness, and respect. The *kibun* factor often plays a decisive role in business because Koreans do not like to give anyone bad news, since such news will obviously damage the recipient's *kibun*. This results in a variety of reactions. Unpleasant news or information may be totally withheld, it may be delayed until near the end of the day to avoid spoiling the person's day, or it may be softened, sometimes to the point that it is misleading.

Koreans especially dislike being the bearer of unpleasant news to someone who has a hot temper and reacts emotionally. They also equate class, breeding, and character with keeping one's emotions under control and responding to any situation calmly and clearly.

In all dealings in Korea, personal and business, it is important to keep this facet of the Korean character in mind, and avoid any unnecessary assaults on anyone's *kibun*.

Facing the World

Another aspect of Korean character (similar to what exists in Japan, China, and other Asian countries), is the concept of "face" and all that it implies. In simple terms, "face" refers to one's social and professional position, and reputation or self-image. It is of extreme importance to Koreans that their "face" be protected and maintained. Anything that threatens or damages their face, whether a comment or an action or even someone's manner, is taken very seriously.

The use of respect language, the extraordinary degree of politeness, the custom of heaping praise on people and of massaging their *kibun* (feelings) are parts of the overall process of avoiding any threat to one's self-image—as a man or a woman, as a competent worker, as a professional, or whatever.

The downside of this cultural characteristic is that people avoid being critical when criticism is due, are excessive in their compliments, and put much more emphasis on form and appearance than on content or underlying reality. This attitude is often misinterpreted by foreigners who are unfamiliar with this kind of behavior, and end up being misled.

The foreign businessman in Korea should keep in mind that while Koreans as a rule are genuinely friendly and

often overly anxious to please, this aspect of their traditional behavior can cause serious problems if the foreigner
presumes that what he sees and hears is what he is going to
get.

The Kindness Trap

Koreans are legendary for their kindness and hospitality. It
is one of their strongest cultural traditions—and is now
used unabashedly in their diplomacy and business with the
rest of the world. Foreign visitors are entertained and pampered, often to the point that they are no longer able to
make objective decisions. This gives Koreans a tremendous
advantage, especially where Americans are concerned,
since we feel such an overwhelming obligation to recipro-
cate by being less critical and more cooperative in helping
them achieve what they want.

Since it is both financially and emotionally difficult for
the foreign visitor to match the generosity of Korean hosts,
it frequently becomes necessary to limit the amount of
hospitality one accepts, and to take extra steps to get even
with some kind of special gift.

4

Aspects of the Korean Way

The Clans Are Alive and Well

The clan system in Korea has survived its evolution into an industrialized society. Throughout all of Korea there are said to be only thirty-nine root clans, with a relatively small number of branches. For example, there are five branches of the Lee clan (which is also spelled Rhee and Yi). The registers of some families go back 2,500 years.

Old Korean hands also say the *Yangbang* society still exists, with those directly related to the historical dynasties making up the hard core of today's top government officials and company executives. Family background therefore plays a vital role in both business and society in Korea today.

The Problem of Names

One of the most unusual aspects of Korean society and one that also plays a vital role in business as well as all other areas of life, is names—people's names. Altogether there are about 273 family names in Korea, *but over half of all Koreans are named Kim, Lee, Pak, or Choi.*

This situation apparently derives from the fact that Korea was founded by the very families whose names became imbued with a sacred quality that was assiduously maintained from one generation to the next. Confucianism incorporated the concept of revering one's ancestors, which further encouraged the maintenance of the family name and negated any inclination to adopt a new surname that would have no history and no honor.

It has also long been the custom for each Korean to have two given names—one a personal name and the other a generational name, chosen by the parents, grandparents, or an onomancer (name-giver). A male generational name is given to the first son born in a family, and a female generational name is given to the first daughter. Thereafter all additional sons and daughters in the family are given the same generational names.

As the family branches out over the generations, the generational names are continued in the male and female lines, so that eventually people who are very distantly related may have a common generational name that goes back to a remote ancestor.

A great deal of thought goes into the selection of both personal names and generational names, and it is still common for parents to seek the help of onomancers. The object is to select a name that fits the child on the basis of the time it was born and the parents' expectations for the child.

Because of the special, almost mystical, role that names play in Korean society, Koreans are very sensitive about their names, and there are numerous taboos about using them. Generally speaking, first names are used only by family members and close school friends. Many older Koreans are so sensitive about their personal names that they do not like to hear other people say them aloud.

Korean women do not change their names when they marry. They may be called by their maiden name, by the title of *puin* (puu-een) "wife" or *ojumoni* (oh-juu-moe-nee) "wife," or as "the wife of Mr. Lee," etc.

To get around the extraordinary problem created by the fact that every other Korean is either Kim, Lee, Pak, or Choi, the Koreans use titles connected with their profession, place of work, and rank. In a large company where there are dozens to hundreds of Lees, Kims, Paks, and Chois who are all managers, they are distinguished by their title (supervisor, manager, general manager, etc.) plus their section or division. If there are two or more Manager Lees in one section they may be referred to as Manager Lee of Production No. 1; Manager Lee of Production No. 2; and so on.

"Names are indeed a horrendous problem," noted long-time Seoul resident Carole Alexander. "In one department [of the Westin Chosun Hotel] we had two Lees. We called one 'Senior Lee' and the other one 'Baby Lee.'"

On the personal side, Koreans also use the areas where they live to identify each other.

Many of the most common names in Korea may be spelled two or three different ways. Some of the syllables making up the Korean language are also pronounced differently by many people, making the names sound different, especially to foreign ears that are not totally sensitized to the variations in the language.

This name situation creates special problems for foreigners who are newly arrived in Korea and try to telephone people they have recently met. Not being aware of the seriousness of the situation, they frequently fail to get or remember the titles and sections or departments of the people concerned, and are therefore unable to identify which Lee, Choi, Pak, or Kim they want to talk to.

Koreans who have been educated abroad or have had substantial experience with Westerners in Korea have become accustomed to foreigners calling them Mr., Mrs., or Miss, and it is becoming more commonplace for them to also use these Western titles when addressing each other, especially when they do not know the individual's proper Korean title.

It is very important for foreign travelers and businessmen visiting Korea to carefully write down the full name, title (if any), and company section of all Koreans whom they might want to call or meet again. On a personal level, it is also wise to get their home addresses and often their position in the family (first or second son or daughter, etc.).

The name problem is one of the primary reasons why name-cards are so important in doing business in Korea.

Adds Carole Alexander: "The sensitivity of Koreans to

the use of first names is a special problem. Before they can make a decision to use a foreign first name, for example, they often have family meetings and discuss the matter endlessly, with a seriousness that astounds the uninitiated foreigner.

"We had one man who worked for us for fifteen years, and was known by everyone as 'Ted.' I met his daughter one day and was amazed to discover that she did not know her father had a foreign nickname."

Commented a veteran foreign businessman: "In my seventeen years in Korea I have been able to develop close, first-name relationships with only five Koreans. I recall that when I first arrived here, the American ambassador advised me that it would take me one year to get to know a Korean, two years before they would accept me (if I didn't make any terrible mistakes), and three years before I would be able to get any work done.

"The ambassador's timetable proved to be painfully accurate. U.S. companies that assign managers here for only two or three years are wasting time and money. Friendship and trust must be built up on both sides, and if it is solid it will last a lifetime. Once you have established this kind of relationship with Koreans, they will never forget you, and will do everything they can to maintain the relationship."

The Founder Spirit in Korea

Much of the dynamism of the Korean economy during the 1960s, 1970s, and 1980s came from the extraordinary spirit, dedication, and drive of the founding fathers of so many of the country's business enterprises, most of which date from the 1950s and 1960s. They had in common a will to succeed, a missionary zeal, and a self-sacrificing dedication that went far beyond the standards of the typically aggressive businessman. They were able to instill much of this same drive and dedication in the executives and labor force they built up to achieve their goals.

These zealous founders did not rely solely on the benefits of the Confucian loyalty and work ethic, however. They also applied a vigorous Korean version of the "'carrot and stick" or, as it is known in Korean, the *Shin sang pil bol,* form of personnel management, or recognition and incentive, with emphasis on "reward and punishment." Winners were pampered and rewarded, while poor performers were subject to harsh disciplinary action.

With the transition from the founders to the second generation of managers, Korean companies began to rely on more traditional approaches, including corporate paternalism that is especially designed to fit the Korean environment. Bonuses, for example, are paid at *kimchi*-making time, *Chusok* (Obon Festival), on the occasion of death in a family, or when school fees have to be paid.

Because of the group orientation of Korean society, Korean companies often apply rewards as well as punishments on a group basis. This has the effect of further forging bonds among the groups, which in turn contributes to closer personal ties and cohesiveness among employees, resulting in greater productivity.

Daewoo's Woo-Choong Kim

Woo-Choong Kim, founder of the Daewoo business empire, epitomizes the spirit, energy, and ambition of Korean businessmen. Kim established Daewoo in 1976 with an initial investment of $18,000. It presently has over 80,000 employees and sales of well over $4 billion a year.

W. C. Kim's own personal creed is that if you work hard, there is no limit to what you can achieve, and it was this philosophy, he says, that helped propel Daewoo ("Great Universe") into the ranks of the world's great enterprises in less than two decades.

Kim (with three associates and a typist) began the company when he was thirty years old, after he had worked for seven years in a medium-sized garment manufacturing and exporting company. He first exported tricot fabrics to Singapore, from where they were re-exported to Indonesia. When Singapore and Indonesia had a falling-out, Kim began exporting directly to Indonesia. Sales went from

$580,000 in 1967 to almost $4 million in 1969. He quickly established a new factory with twenty lines of sewing capacity, installed quality-control equipment identical to that used by Sears, then opened sales offices in Singapore, London, and New York.

Sears was impressed with Kim's new facilities and prices, and became his first major customer. J. C. Penney, Montgomery Ward, and other large retail chains quickly followed suit. Growth was unbelievably rapid. In 1972, Daewoo was awarded thirty percent of the U.S. total import quota for textile products. By 1975, Daewoo was one of Korea's most profitable firms, and had begun a frenzy of acquisitions, quickly buying fourteen companies and taking major positions in two other firms. In 1976, the Korean government asked Daewoo to go into heavy industry manufacturing, first by taking over the ailing Hankook Machinery Co., which had not made a profit in its thirty-eight-year history.

Kim took personal charge of the new acquisition, often sleeping at the factory. He changed the name of the company to Daewoo Heavy Industries, broke even the first year, and began paying dividends the second year. His reputation as a miracle manager established, Kim subsequently arranged backing to take over other companies, including Korea Steel Chemical Company, Saehan Motor Company, and Okpo Shipbuilding Company.

Kim was born in 1936 during the Japanese occupation of Korea. His father was a professor and his mother a university graduate, when it was extremely rare for a woman to attend college. He had three brothers and one sister. In 1950, when Communist troops from North Korea overran Seoul, he saw his father and uncle abducted, and was never to hear from or see them again. He was thirteen at the time. The only source of income for the family was what he earned as a newspaper delivery boy.

Recalling this period to an interviewer years later, he said: "One evening I came home exhausted and hungry. There was only a single bowl of rice available for the five of us. I said that I had already eaten. My mother told the younger children to eat the rice, claiming that she had also eaten. Then each in turn urged the other to eat the rice.

Suddenly, we looked at each other, hugged, and burst into tears. That was the happiest moment in my life."

Following the end of the Korean War, Kim managed to enter and graduate from Yonsei University, holding down part-time jobs to cover his living expenses. His only hobby, he said, was hard work, which to him meant working sixteen hours a day, 365 days a year.

In 1983, during a program to revitalize the managerial spirit of the Daewoo empire, Kim told his employees:

"Creativity comes from hard work. To become wise, it's not how many books you read but how much you concentrate in your reading that is important. Business is the same. Traveling around the world, I can see money everywhere. It is in the streets and in the houses. It is in America and in Africa. It is everywhere, but you have to work hard to see it and to get it. If you try hard enough, you will see more money than you could possibly collect in the time you have.

"Ten years ago we were a small company, but even then we felt a sense of challenge to become an important factor in our national scene. Since we had little money, the only way for us to grow was to rescue seriously troubled companies. And this we did by showing the workers what it meant to work hard.

"Many people point to the Japanese management system as the reason for their success. But what can a system do without good people? You need people who are dedicated and experienced. The only advantage the Japanese firm has over a Korean firm is the experience of its people. You take shipbuilding, for example. The Japanese welder has twenty years' experience and our Korean welder has two years' experience. But that advantage will lessen over time.

"The American company is not what it used to be. In the old days, Americans worked hard to challenge new frontiers. But as their economy got mature, they became more interested in nice houses, jogging, and having a good time than in doing business. How can you compete without dedication? It is not the management system that is not working in American companies, it is the people not working hard.

"Korea is no exception to this cycle of hard work. As the

standard of living improves in Korea, we shall eventually lose the spirit of working hard. Until we get to that stage, we have to keep our economy growing."

Kim later added: "I know my strength as an entrepreneur. I also know my weakness as an organization builder. I can be an asset for Daewoo so long as it grows rapidly, and a liability when it needs to be stabilized. When that time comes, I shall resign as chairman and hand over the job to a manager capable of structuring managerial systems in the group. Once my successor accomplishes his task, it will be time for him to turn over the chairmanship to someone else with entrepreneurial skills. From then, entrepreneurial leadership would operate through a coordinated system."

In 1980, three years before the revitalization program was launched, Kim donated all of his personal holdings in Daewoo Corporation to a foundation dedicated to helping the Korean people. At that time he said: "When a businessman begins to count his wealth, his life as a businessman comes to an end. Profits are for reinvestment, not for enjoyment." He added that successful businessmen had a responsibility to become national leaders, and only those who were willing to sacrifice their personal interests could truly take on such leadership roles.

Daewoo's Woo-Bock Lee, one of the founding members, says the single most important factor in the giant conglomerate's success was its commitment to its employees. "We believe every person has potential. If a person is doing poorly, we start with the assumption that the company is not employing that person where he could show his talents. In line with this belief, we have never fired anyone from an acquired company. We work hard to motivate these people," he said.

Lee added that in 1976 Daewoo began recruiting well-educated Americans and Europeans, and a few years later began sending twenty to thirty engineers and managers abroad each year for advanced study. At that time, Chairman Kim announced that Daewoo would soon have over a thousand scientists and engineers with Ph.D.'s.

Summed up Ho-Min Yoo, a managing director of

Daewoo Corporation: "The spirit of being in a family has made this company what it is. Every employee receives a present on his or her birthday. If employees are sick at home or at the hospital, their boss and fellow workers visit them just like relatives. Chairman Kim stays overnight at the home of a Daewoo executive on the eve of a parent's funeral (a Korean custom for one's relatives and close friends).

"When one of our general managers was killed in the tragic downing of a Korean airliner by the Soviet military near Murmansk in 1978, he was promoted posthumously to the rank of director, his wife was awarded seventy percent of his salary for the rest of her life, and his children received scholarships for college. We think of ourselves more as the Daewoo family than the Daewoo group."

The Daewoo Group consists of twenty-five of the largest companies in Korea, including the so-called Big Five— Daewoo Corporation, Daewoo Heavy Industries Ltd., Daewoo Shipbuilding and Heavy Machinery Ltd., Daewoo Motor Company, and Daewoo Electronics Company.

Korean-American Business Institute (KABI)

An organization that is of special interest to foreign and Korean businessmen alike is the Korean-American Business Institute, established in 1974 by Woo-Joo Chang as a nonprofit organization aimed at providing education, research, consultation, and cooperation in the field of international business, particularly cross-cultural management training that provides the insights and management skills needed to do business in Korea.

The KABI (Rm 808, Paik Nam Building, 188-3 Eul-Chi Ro, 10-ga, Seoul) sponsors an annual seminar on the various aspects of doing business in Korea. The seminars are usually held in the fall.

The transition that Korea has made from a feudalistic, unindustrialized society to one of the dozen or so top industrial powers in the world in just two decades is epitomized by KABI founder Woo-Joo Chang. Born in what is now North Korea, Chang fled southward in the winter of 1945 to escape from the communist regime imposed on the north by the Russians.

After a long journey on foot, Chang, another student, and a young woman who had joined them just half an hour before reached the northern bank of the Hantan River at about 4:30 A.M. on the morning of December 10, 1945. The three began wading across the icy river.

Seven Russian soldiers who had been hiding in foliage along the riverbank suddenly stood up, pointed their rifles at the three, and yelled for them to stop. The soldiers told the three that they could not go south, then robbed them of their money, watches, and rings. The soldiers then told Chang and the other male student they could go, and led the girl back into the bushes. Chang continues the story.

"When we got near the middle of the icy river, where the water was chest high, the soldiers fired on us. There was no way we could escape so we turned around facing them and raised our hands. But they signaled for us to go on. We finished crossing the river walking backwards, with our hands in the air.

"We continued southward as fast as we could go, expecting any moment to run into 'Yankee' or American soldiers. To us, 'Yankee' meant 'Western ghosts who sip blood.'

"About a mile from the river we spotted some American soldiers in the distance. One of them seemed to be holding a submachine gun on the men and women refugees who were walking by him. They are robbing the people, just like the Russians, we thought. We had nothing more to give and needless to say, approached the Americans with a great deal of trepidation.

"As we drew closer we found that the American soldier was not holding a gun but a DDT sprayer. The Americans demanded nothing of us. After spraying each one of us, the soldier said 'OK,' indicating that we could go on.

"That was my first encounter with the West, and it had a great impact on my life. My preconceived notions of 'Western ghosts' quickly gave way to new concepts of human decency, justice, and honor. The misconceptions I had had caused much undue anxiety, mistrust, and fear."

Following his escape from Soviet-dominated North Korea, the young Woo-Joo Chang went on to attend the Korean Military Academy, the U.S. Command and General Staff College, the National Defense College, and Harvard Business School.

His career included serving as Dean of Faculty for the National Defense College, Commanding General of the 3rd Infantry Division, Senior Korean Delegate to the Military Armistice Commission of the United Nations Command, Assistant Minister of Defense for Comptroller, Deputy Chief of Staff for Plans and Policy at Army Headquarters, International President of the Korean Construction Corporation, President of Hyundai Corporation, President of Hyundai Construction Company, and President of Halla Construction Company.

Chang added that many people in the business world today still suffer from the influence of serious misconceptions and that it was the goal of the KABI to rid people of cross-cultural fears and anxieties and to make it possible for them to better understand each other.

5

Dealing with "Big Brother"

The Government Role

Korean commentators disagree with the foreign use of the term Korea Inc., which they say is misleading. They explain that the influence of the government on business can hardly be exaggerated, but that the influence is both positive and negative. They maintain that government laws, regulations, and red tape are more obstructive than helpful, particularly where smaller enterprises are concerned because they are often prevented from taking advantage of entrepreneurial opportunities.

Said a foreign businessman resident in Seoul: "The government is everywhere. Government officials even check on whether or not hotel employees have been taught how to bow properly."

In whatever area or perspective, the influence of the government on the operations of foreign businesses in Korea is especially significant. The legal basis for business relations between the U.S. and Korea is a treaty signed in 1956.

The U.S.–Korea Treaty of Friendship, Commerce, and Navigation

On November 28, 1956, the U.S. and Korea signed a Treaty of Friendship, Commerce, and Navigation, which was designed to accord each other "national treatment" and "most favored nation" privileges.

Under this agreement, National Treatment (NT) specifies that each country will treat the citizens and products of the other country the same as it does its own. Most Favored Nation Treatment (MFNT) specifies that each country will treat the citizens and products of the other country with no less favorable terms than they treat the people and products of third nations in their respective countries.

The specific provisions covered by the treaty include general treatment, physical access, personal rights, employment rules, due process, property protection, enterprise rights, engagement of foreign specialists, leasing (not ownership) of real estate and immovable property and the purchasing and leasing of movable property, intangible property protection, MFNT regarding payments and fund transfers, the right to bring in product samples, and to engage in importing and exporting with MFNT.

Many other treaty provisions add to the "rights" guaranteed to the citizens of each country. Unfortunately, in the case of Korea, many of these rights are ignored totally and others are blatantly abused.

Among the treaty provisions most abused are those ostensibly permitting the establishment and operation of all types of businesses (wholesale companies, retail operations, and for all practical purposes, trading companies, cannot be established by foreigners); product samples cannot be brought in freely; and there is open discrimination in the application of customs duties. It is difficult or impossible to remit profits, dividends, and royalties, etc.

Says the American Chamber of Commerce in Korea: "There is a substantial disregard of the terms of the TFCN, and these affect a broad spectrum of U.S. [and other foreign] enterprises operating in and attempting to operate in Korea."

Following the Leader

In the ROK the national interest takes precedence over private business, and the government plays a key role in most industries by significantly influencing or outright controlling who can do what and how it is done. The government exercises its influence and control through a variety of laws, long precedent, and the willing cooperation and support of much of the Korean business community.

The objective of the Korean government is to do everything possible to encourage the rapid and rational growth of the economy and development of the national infrastructure so the entire nation benefits, rather than allow a free-for-all atmosphere which results in extraordinary growth in some areas but disruptions or deteriorations in others.

Within the context of this overall government policy, individual businessmen and enterprises are allowed the freedom to grow as fast as they can and make as much profit as possible. To keep industrial and social development going forward in the direction it desires, the government makes ready use of all of its powers.

Some of the methods used by the government—and by Korean companies in their dealings with foreign partners—to get its way are to impose import or export restrictions, to deny or delay licensing applications, to cause customs clearance difficulties, to refuse to renew visas, to stop payments, to break contracts, and so on.

Despite the real and apparent handicaps this policy represents to foreign companies wanting to do business in Korea, the overall climate for foreign investment and business activity in Korea is favorable, and offers special opportunities to those who are able and willing to approach the market with an open mind, goodwill, a great deal of flexibility, determination, and patience.

At the same time, there are many Korean businessmen, government officials, and others who are strongly opposed to welcoming any more foreign businessmen in the country because of potential danger to its security and continuing economic success—in direct contradiction to the public policies of the government.

These sentiments are often responsible for the "invisible barriers" that foreign businessmen frequently encounter in Korea.

Because these conflicting positions and practices further

complicate the relationship between businessmen and government, it is vital that the foreign businessman who hopes to succeed in Korea understand the psychology of Korean behavior and master some of the techniques for dealing with individuals on many levels in a variety of different ministries or agencies.

The first and probably most important lesson the foreign businessman must learn is that individual government officials cannot be approached on a strictly rational, practical, or policy basis. Everything is handled on a case-by-case and very personal basis. Furthermore, officials on different levels in the same agencies and ministries will interpret the same laws and factors differently, often resulting in substantial delays before an application or proposal can be steered through the government red tape.

Probably the second most important lesson is that neither the ethical nor the legal system in Korea provides the kind or depth of security and protection that the typical Western businessman is used to and expects. This includes the view and treatment of contracts, patents, copyrights, and other legal matters.

The third most important lesson may well be that even after everything has been approved and seems to be in order, the whole thing can come apart and have to be renegotiated because, in the view of some government official or company executive, circumstances have changed and the original agreement is no longer valid.

This means, of course, that the successful businessman in Korea must remain in constant communication with everyone even remotely connected or involved in his business, in order to remain current on their thinking and plans and to be able to anticipate their actions.

Again this comes down to establishing and nurturing personal relations with company managers and government officials on all the appropriate levels in all the concerned ministries or agencies. This entails a great deal of one's personal time as well as expenditures for drinks, meals, and other expenses. The developing and nurturing of personal relations of this type cannot be done casually or taken for granted. It is a serious business.

Another aspect of the personal side of business in Korea

is that the foreign businessman, no matter what his experience or credentials in his home country, must "re-prove" himself in Korea in terms that are acceptable to Koreans. He must earn the respect and loyalty of Korean associates and employees through his professional skills and knowledge, through his approach to developing and maintaining the expected personal relations, by not breaking any of the taboos of Korean society, by demonstrating sincerity and appreciation for Korean sensitivities, etc.

It is especially important for the foreign employer in Korea to treat his Korean staff with enlightened, personal concern that keeps them loyal and motivated. This includes following expected procedures in management and otherwise dealing with employees.

The Red Tape Syndrome

Bureaucratic red tape in Korea is formidable, and affects both domestic and foreign operations. In one application for a joint venture involving pharmaceuticals, the various government ministries and agencies required 312 documents covering sixty-two administrative procedures, and taking two years and nine months to prepare. (Korea is not alone in its obsession with red tape. The same application in Japan requires 325 documents and forty-six administrative procedures. The same step in the U.S. requires twenty-three documents and nine administrative procedures.)

Among the documents needed in Korea: a description of the investment plan, evidence of proxy authority, a certificate of nationality, specifications of foreign capital to be introduced, the joint-venture agreement, and documentation showing that the applicants will subscribe to stocks and shares.

High Military Profile

The military is a conspicuous aspect of life in Korea, with significant influence in politics, education, private industry, and society in general, just as it was during the country's long feudal dynasties.

Because of the ongoing threat from Communist North Korea, the ROK has been on a high military alert status since the ending of the Korean War in 1953. All eligible males must register for the draft and, with few exceptions, undergo military training and spend time in the reserves. Government regulations about military service are rigorously enforced. The government will not hire adult males who have not completed their military training. They may also be denied the right to obtain a passport and travel abroad.

The military training system is very thorough and tough, with strict discipline that later carries over into civilian life. There is great prestige in being selected for schooling at a military academy and going on to a career as a military officer. Those who succeed in reaching the higher ranks are invariably assured of equally prestigious positions in government or with private industry after they retire.

Most foreign businesses in the ROK accommodate themselves to this situation and attempt to see the positive side. Generally speaking, the foreign business community supports the position of the government that North Korea poses a direct military threat to the ROK. There is also a general consensus that the militaristic bent of Koreans has been a major contributing factor in the economic advances made by the ROK since the 1960s.

The reference here, of course, is to the fact that Korean companies and the various government agencies marshal and manage their manpower very much like military organizations, and plot their strategy and tactics with the precision and purpose that is characteristic of military campaigns. They also demand the same kind of loyalty, commitment, and sacrifices that are typical of the military in do-or-die situations.

The Most Important Ministry

It is essential that the foreign businessman in Korea familiarize himself with the Ministry of Finance (MOF), which has jurisdiction over virtually every area or phase of business that pertains to foreign businesses operating in the country. These areas of business include the monetary system, banking, national taxes, national tariffs, foreign exchange, foreign economic cooperation, and property of the state and government financial accounting.

The MOF also interprets and administers the Foreign Capital Inducement Law (FCIL) and the Foreign Exchange Control Law (FECL).

The MOF is made up of eight bureaus and agencies, along with four external organizations.

The bureaus and agencies are:

Customs and Tariff Bureau
Economic Cooperation Bureau
Finance Bureau
International Finance Bureau
Planning and Management Office
Securities and Insurance Bureau
Tax Bureau
Treasury Bureau

The external organizations controlled by the Ministry of Finance are the Customs Administration, National Banks, Monopoly Administration, and the Office of National Tax Administration.

The Customs and Tariff Bureau administers customs and tariffs regulations, and controls the entry of foreign goods into Korea through its tariff and nontariff barriers.

The Economic Cooperation Bureau administers the Foreign Investment Control Law, which controls foreign investment in Korea, the inflow and outflow of foreign exchange, and all foreign economic cooperation. The Finance Bureau controls the banking system, the nonbanking financial system, and all financial policy.

The International Finance Bureau is in charge of the ROK's foreign exchange policy, international finance, and overseas investment. The Office of National Tax Administration includes a direct tax bureau, an indirect tax bureau, a collection and appeals bureau, and an investigative bureau. All tax assessments, collections, changes, exemptions, etc., are controlled by this agency.

The Powerful MTI

Korea's Ministry of Trade and Industry (MTI) is credited with being the second most important government entity as far as businessmen are concerned. It has jurisdiction over all manufacturing and trading of goods as well as after-sales services; it issues export licenses, sets import controls, has jurisdiction over the administration of patents, controls all government technical assistance programs, reviews the contents of technology inducement contracts—and requests changes in the contracts when it sees fit to do so. The MTI indirectly controls the Small and Medium Industry Development Corporation, the Korean Trade Promotion (KOTRA), Korean Traders Association (KTA), and the Korean Chamber of Commerce and Industry (KCCI).

The Ministry of Trade and Industry also uses its power to play a key role in the application of nontariff barriers against foreign products to either limit their importation or keep them out of the country entirely.

MTI is made up of nine bureaus and offices:

Basic Industry Bureau
Electronic Industry and Electrical Appliance Industry
  Bureau
Free Export Zone Administrative Office
International Trade Promotion Bureau
Machinery Industry Bureau
Planning and Management Office
Small and Medium Industry Bureau
Textile and Consumer Goods Industry Bureau
Trade Bureau

Another government body of special concern to the foreign businessman in Korea is the Ministry of Labor (MOL), which is made up of the Labor Policy Bureau, Labor Stan-

Theodore Lownik Library
Illinois Benedictine College
Lisle, Illinois 60532

dards Bureau, Employment Security Bureau, Labor Insurance Bureau, Planning and Management Office, and the Vocational Training Bureau.

The MOL has jurisdiction over all labor affairs in the country, including work rules, working conditions, labor welfare, workmen's compensation insurance, vocational training, employment security, and labor dispute mediation.

Labor policy making, wages, welfare, labor unions, and labor/management consultations come under the jurisdiction of the Labor Policy Bureau. Working conditions, industrial safety, and work rules for women and minors are controlled by the Labor Standards Bureau.

The Federation of Korean Industries

The Federation of Korean Industries (FKI) is of importance because its members represent the largest and most powerful companies in the country, and when they act in concert their influence is overwhelming. Founded in 1961, the FKI presently has 427 members. The criteria for membership are annual sales of forty billion *won* or more in industry and commerce, and funding of one billion *won* or more in research.

The charter of the FKI calls for it to maintain relations with similar international organizations and institutions, to promote the development of technological research and industry, to promote cooperation between business and academia, and to promote overseas investment and cooperation with foreign countries.

In one sense, the FKI represents Korea Inc. The behavior of many of its members, in fact, works to limit the entry and activities of foreign firms rather than aid them.

Laws Are Not Binding

Koreans do not regard laws as representing either guidelines or principles on which their society is based. Confucian precepts remain the basic guidelines of their attitudes and practices, and laws are merely a device of the government to restrict their behavior—or at the most, to remind people of their duty. Koreans almost never resort to the law or to courts to resolve disputes. They regard such an action as an ultimate breach of etiquette and civilized behavior, and thereafter refuse to have anything to do with anyone guilty of such unacceptable conduct.

Lawyers in Korea do not look upon themselves as owing their primary allegiance to a client. Their view of their obligation and role is not individualized in this manner. They see their job in a holistic sense—"to protect human rights and realize social justice," in the words of their credo. In other words, they put the welfare of Korean society in general (and by extension, the country itself) above the interests of individual clients.

This is virtually the opposite of both the philosophy and behavior of Western lawyers, who characteristically put their own interests first and their clients' second, and seldom concern themselves with the interests of their country (unless they are being paid by the government for their services).

It is much easier to understand the behavior of Korean attorneys when it is considered that traditionally they were officials of the court and acted only on behalf of the court. The idea of their taking an adversary position against the government or against a Korean company or giving business advice to a corporation is still a new experience.

Although there is a fairly large number of foreign attorneys in Korea, they are not permitted to practice law directly. They are employed as members of Korean law firms for obvious reasons—their foreign-language skills, their knowledge of foreign law, and their ability to attract and deal with foreign clients in their own cultural context.

Korean law firms are structured in the same hierarchical manner as most Korean organizations, with power concentrated in the hands of one or two people at the top. This usually means that matters of any importance must receive the attention of these senior attorneys. Foreign businessmen should keep in mind that the Western attorneys in

Korean law offices are very limited in what they can do, and their backgrounding in Korean law is often relatively limited.

The Law and Business

Attorneys in Korea note that the legal foundation in the country is based on the German system of civil law, and that it is not nearly as flexible as the law in the United States and England. Precedent has less to do with the interpretation of law, and judges are more likely to follow the letter of the law. But there is a growing tendency for trial courts to attempt to comply with decisions handed down by higher courts to avoid reversals of their rulings.

The most important government regulation applying to business, according to attorneys, is the Foreign Exchange Control Act (FECA), which controls the receipt and remittance of money in and out of Korea, along with contractual agreements regarding such currency transactions. A main point is that foreign companies planning on doing business in Korea should obtain government approval for receiving or remitting funds prior to beginning business. If approval is obtained in advance, later transactions should be more or less automatic.

What Kind of Operation Is Best?

There are four kinds of business operations in Korea that may be used by the foreign businessman: an agency relationship, a liaison or representative office, a branch office, or various forms of a corporation. Appointing an agent is the easiest and most informal approach to the Korean market. But an agent cannot engage in profit-making activities on behalf of the client, and cannot remit profits out of Korea. Generally, agents are limited to gathering information, performing research, placing advertising, or buying goods which are shipped to the client.

An agent can conclude a contract for a foreign client and

can engage in sales on behalf of a client, but the income earned on such sales may be subject to Korean taxes. If the agent is independent and acting on its own, it may conduct tax-exempt sales for a foreign supplier.

One way around this independent agency requirement is to engage an agent who also represents several other foreign clients and is therefore not an exclusive agent for one company.

A liaison or representative office can be opened in Korea without registering with the district court or tax office, but a report of the opening should be filed with the Bank of Korea in order to facilitate foreign exchange transactions. The liaison office cannot engage in income-producing activity, and because it is not a legal entity, all of the assets of the office must be in the name of the representative. This latter requirement has caused considerable problems in the past when foreign companies appointed representatives without carefully investigating them, had a falling-out, and then could not recover the assets of the office.

A branch office becomes a legal presence in Korea, and can own assets and conduct business activities for profit, but its activities become taxable under Korean law. If the branch office activities are limited to purchasing, arranging for third-party processing of products, storing goods not for sale, or engaging in other nonprofit activities, it may be exempt from taxes. On the other hand, if a branch or individual concludes contracts on behalf of a principal or receives orders or deliveries from a principal, they become subject to taxation.

Bank of Korea (BOK) approval is necessary to open a branch office in Korea, requiring a formal application and a number of specific documents that include a business plan and the scope of business you intend to pursue. The branch must also be registered with the Court Registration Office and the Tax Office.

Whether or not an application to open a branch in Korea is approved is determined by the type of activity you want to engage in. Generally speaking, branch offices seeking to engage in manufacturing are denied, since manufacturing operations come under the Ministry of Finance.

If you request remittance privileges when establishing a branch, and the application is approved, you cannot remit any profits for the first three years, and during the next five years are limited to an annual remittance of not more than twenty percent of the foreign funds brought into the country to establish the branch.

There are several other requirements applying to the setting up and operating of a branch office, one of the most important of which is reporting all operating funds brought into the country to the Bank of Korea.

The fourth type of presence in Korea is the company— of which there are four kinds: the *hapmyung hoesa* (hop-myung hoe-eh-sah) or partnership; the *hapcha hoesa* (hop-chah hoe-eh-sah) or limited partnership; the *chusik hoesa* (chuu-sheek hoe-eh-sah) or stock company; and the *yuhan hoesa* (yuu-hahn hoe-eh-sah) or limited liability company.

Some ninety percent of all Korean companies are *chusik hoesa,* or stock companies, which are similar to American stock companies, and only this form plus occasionally the *yuhan hoesa,* or limited liability company, is recommended for foreign businessmen. One of the limitations of the *yuhan hoesa* is that it can have a maximum of only fifty share-holders, but the fact that restrictions on the transfer of its shares can be legally enforced is sometimes attractive to the foreign investor.

The minimum capital required to form a corporation in Korea is fifty million *won,* and shares generally must have a minimum par value of five thousand *won.* Shares valued at less than five thousand *won* can be sold only with court approval. Some other characteristics of Korean stock companies: a corporation generally cannot buy its own shares; if forty percent or more of the shares of a subsidiary are owned by the parent company, the subsidiary cannot acquire the shares of its parent; dividends can be issued in cash or shares, but the latter is limited to fifty percent of any one dividend; interim dividends are not permitted.

The Korean side of joint ventures sometimes refuses to vote for dividend distribution, either because they want to reinvest the profits in the company or because they are prevented from doing so because of the financial situation of their parent company. It is therefore important that the JV dividend policy be clearly established during the formation of the joint venture.

The Finance Minister maintains a list of Korean businesses that are not open to foreign investment. Any industry not included on this list is eligible for foreign investment, either wholly owned, in a joint venture, or through stock acquisition. Government policy favors small and medium-sized enterprises, however, and large foreign firms may not be permitted to enter an eligible industry except via a joint venture with another firm already in that industry. An exception may be made if the large foreign company plans to produce something in Korea that cannot be made by existing companies.

The higher the percentage of foreign ownership in a joint-venture application, the closer scrutiny the application gets from the Ministry of Finance. Upon receiving applications for the entry of foreign firms, the MOF refers them to the ministry in charge of that industry category.

There are many conditions, some written and some unwritten, that the MOF and other ministries apply during the process of reviewing applications for setting up foreign operations in Korea. One example: in the case of a fifty-fifty joint venture, the director elected by the foreign partner cannot have the right to break a tie vote.

It is important that the foreign company seeking to establish an operation in Korea monitor the application review process as it passes through the various ministries and agencies, taking advantage of every opportunity to respond to negative reactions and add additional explanations and arguments for its approval.

At present the minimum initial foreign investment in a new company in Korea is U.S. $100,000. There is no maximum limit. Foreign individuals working for Foreign Invested Companies (FIC) are exempt from personnel income taxes for the first five years of the life of the company. FICs that make a major contribution to the Korean economy may also be exempt from taxes.

Licensing Foreign Technology

Licensing of foreign technology in Korea, commonly referred to as Technical Assistance Agreements (TAA), comes under the Foreign Capital Inducement Act (FCIA) and is reviewed by the Fair Trade Commission of the Economic Planning Bureau (EPB). The EPB has a specific list of so-called unfair practices against which it measures all TAA applications. The Bureau also has a model license agreement which, if used, does not require review by the FTC.

The FCIA will not accept licensing applications covering designs or brands, low-level or out-of-date technology, or those that are judged to be primarily attempts to sell raw materials, parts, or accessories, or that involve an industry that is on the protected list.

Other ministries involved in the approval of TAA have their own guidelines that may vary widely, but the one on which most of them agree is holding the level of royalties to no more than five percent. The more desirable the technology, the higher the royalty rate the government is likely to approve.

Two crucial points foreign businessmen should keep in mind: the Korean government views the licensing of technology as a technology transfer, and the Korean licensee has rights to the unregistered technology that survives termination of the agreement. Exceptions to this are if the licensee terminates the agreement prematurely or if the use of the technology would infringe on the licensor's registered property rights.

As the TAA designation directly implies, the Korean government regards licensing as technical assistance agreements, and the idea is for the licensee to obtain all the available know-how regarding the technology during the life of the agreement, making renewal of the agreement unnecessary. In practice, however, the renewal of licensing agreements is fairly easy in most cases, at this time. Royalty payments are exempt from taxes for the first five years, unless the exemption is waived.

Importing and Exporting Licenses

Importing and exporting come under the Foreign Trade Transaction Act (FTTA). Licenses must be obtained from the appropriate agency. There are several kinds of licenses but the two most common are a general trading license and a special trading license. To be eligible for a general trading license, a company must have a minimum paid-in capital of one hundred million *won,* and must show that it has either exported goods valued at $200,000 or more, manufactured goods for export valued at $300,000 or more in the previous six months, or has processed goods for a fee of $100,000 or more. The general trading license must be renewed annually, and to be eligible for renewal the company has to export a minimum of $500,000 worth of goods each year.

Special trading licenses do not require export performances and permit the Korean holder to import anything that is not on a prohibited or restricted list.

Foreign companies in Korea are eligible for both general and special trading licenses if they meet the requirements. Foreign branches in Korea may obtain a special trading license without meeting export performance requirements, but they can import only products that are made by their parent company or its affiliate, and the imported product has to be used for stock sales in Korea.

Exporting from Korea is a lot freer than importing into the country. With a proper license, a trading company can export anything not prohibited. Foreign-invested firms that manufacture in Korea may export everything they make.

Product Classification and Eligibility

Korea classifies all products under the Customs Cooperations Council Nomenclature (CCCN) system, which is based on industry classifications. For the purposes of import control, products are further classified as prohibited, restricted, or automatic approval products ("AA").

Products that are prohibited cannot, of course, be imported into the country. Those on the restricted list require special approval from the appropriate ministry or trade association. At the present time, approximately 950 products are on the restricted list, and whether or not they are approved upon special application is determined by the private industry association designated by the Ministry of Trade and Industry as having jurisdiction over that product.

Korea's liberalized import ratio is approaching the ninety-five percent mark, which is said to be about the same as most advanced nations.

Customs Duties

All imported products are subject to customs duties, which are based on the quality and quantity of the items at the time of import declaration. When the transaction is between related parties, the duty is not based on the invoice price but on what customs officials judge to be the true value. The law allows customs officials to apply up to a forty percent surcharge on imports to "stabilize prices or discourage the importation of particular goods."

Lawyers

The general consensus is that good attorneys are available in Korea, including both foreign and Korean. The point is also made that several of the Korean attorneys available in Seoul have degrees from foreign universities. "They have become very skilled at working both sides of the fence in joint-venture matters, and can be of vital importance to the foreign company," said one experienced expatriate.

Big Brother in the Newsroom

The news media in Korea traditionally worked under strict government regulations that make it difficult or impossible to report all of the news without fear or favor. One of the political reforms announced in June 1987 was freedom of the press. But even if this is fully realized, Korean newsmen themselves tend to interpret the news they publish from a strongly nationalistic bias. The influence of the government is such that much of the news is slanted to suit its purposes.

The foreign businessman operating in Korea quickly becomes aware of both the government influence and the Korean bias of local media, and makes certain he has access to several other sources of information.

Copyright Protection

In December 1986, the Korean legislature accepted the Section 301 Agreement with the U.S., covering insurance and intellectual property rights, including foreign-created books, songs, software, drugs, and other products. The agreement became law on July 1, 1987. Two months later, Korea signed the Universal Copyright Convention.

Under this law, selected foreign product inventions involving chemicals, pharmaceuticals, and their derivatives, but not foods or beverages, can be patented in Korea for a period of fifteen years from the date of publication or registration. American product patent applications pending on July 1, 1987, came under protection retroactively. The law does not apply to products being manufactured in Korea prior to July 1, 1987.

Foreign books, written and published abroad after July 1, 1987, are protected during the life of the author plus fifty years. Recordings are protected for twenty years. The copyright protection law does not apply to books published before July 1, 1987.

Korea's Labor Laws

Korea's Labor Union Law authorizes and protects collective bargaining, but only unions organized according to the statutory process are entitled to recognition and protection. The Ministry of Labor has the power to cancel or amend the bylaws of any union that it views as posing a threat to the public interest. All members of a union must be directly employed by the company, and interference by outsiders is strictly prohibited. Workers cannot be forced to join a union. Employers cannot refuse to bargain, subsidize a union, dismiss an employee for giving evidence about the violation of a law, or penalize a union member or oganizer.

Before a union can call a strike it must have a majority vote by the union members, file a report of intention to strike with the appropriate government agency, and take a thirty-day cooling-off period.

All employers with five or more employees must provide them with insurance covering medical expenses, lay-offs, disability, and funeral expenses, as designated by the Industrial Accident Compensation Insurance Law.

Korea has ten laws that apply to labor and to varying degrees must be a part of every employment package. The most important of these laws is the basic Labor Standards Law, which specifies working hours, conditions, severance pay, etc., and covers such things as mandatory documents that must exist, employment contracts, rules of employment, termination, severance pay, vacations, bonuses, and other allowances.

The other nine laws are:

Labor Union Law
Labor Dispute Adjustment Law
Special Law Concerning Labor Unions and Labor Dispute Adjustment for Foreign Invested Enterprises
Labor Committee Law
Labor-Management Council Law
Industrial Accident Compensation Insurance Law
Industrial Safety and Health Law
Basic Law for Vocational Training
Employment Security Law

The provisions of these laws are very specific and detailed. Translations of the laws are available from the

American Chamber of Commerce in Korea, and it is imperative that Western businessmen wanting to do business in Korea obtain copies of the laws, along with advice on what parts of the laws apply particularly to their operation.

A spokesman for the Chamber states bluntly: "ROK companies often do not follow these laws, but foreign firms must!"

Labeling Requirements

As of 1985, all foreign products imported into Korea must be labeled in the Korean language. There are specific requirements for different products, and these must be followed precisely before the item will be cleared through customs.

Minimum Pricing

Another law that went into effect in 1985 was one establishing a minimum price for which imported goods can be sold in Korea. This price is fixed by the Korean government on a case-by-case basis. The stated reason for this law is to prevent dumping in Korea, but the minimum price set by the government often bears no relation to the production cost or the foreign sales price of the item.

Land Ownership in Korea

The Alien Land Acquisition Law states that foreign companies may purchase land in Korea for the construction of necessary facilities upon receiving approval from the Ministry of Home Affairs. In practice, however, the ministry has never approved any land purchase application by any foreign company. This factor alone adds tremendously to the cost of doing business in Korea, since rents are very high.

6

Major Problem Areas

View of the U.S.

There is a strong tendency for Koreans to see themselves as much harder workers than most Westerners, Americans in particular, and to discredit the ability of Americans to make sacrifices for their families or their country. This attitude was exemplified by a woman who had put her sister through a college in the U.S. by working as a maid. "You Americans can't do things like that," she said.

The extraordinary success of its export industries has also convinced most Koreans that Korean-made products are superior to products made in the U.S.—in the same kind of turnaround that occurred in Japan during the 1960s.

At the same time, there is still great respect and feelings of gratitude toward Americans (except among student and political radicals who continue to disapprove of the American presence in Korea). One of the special ways this gratitude is officially recognized is a law that makes it possible for Americans who served in Korea during the war to own property in the country.

Foreign Managers in Korea

"American companies entering Korea today are no better informed, no wiser than they were in the 1960s and 1970s.

60

They still assign junior executives with little knowledge of the country, and less experience. They shove these young men into an alien world, expecting them to perform on the basis of their knowledge of the companies' American operations, said Marvin Winship, a consultant and executive recruiting specialist with years of business experience in Korea.

"One of the toughest experiences of my years in Korea was running a joint venture in which the head office was trying to impose their way on the Korean side. Attempting to convince the top executives in the U.S. that the operation had to be tailored to fit the Korean environment was one of the worst ordeals I've ever experienced."

Winship said that many young American managers sent to Korea have ended up having nervous breakdowns when they were unable to convert the Koreans over to their way of doing business.

The Big Company Syndrome

The bigger the American company, the more likely it is to get into trouble in Korea. Lee Iacocca and his top people came in several times and made no effort at all to take advantage of the accumulated experience and wisdom of the American Chamber of Commerce (Amcham) in Seoul.

The Chrysler people spent a lot of time and money trying to talk Samsung, the electronics manufacturer, into going into the production of automobiles. There were already four automobile manufacturers in Korea at that time and there was no way the government was going to let a fifth company enter the field. Samsung wouldn't let on that what Chrysler wanted was impossible because it hoped the government would make an exception of its policy and let them do it. Chrysler is said to have spent millions before they gave up, and went with Hyundai.

If the Chrysler people had had the common sense to visit Amcham they could have learned this lesson for nothing, and saved a great deal of time, frustration, and ill will. Said a local businessman: "It was incredible that they didn't talk to a single person in Seoul to get their advice or help."

Eventually, of course, Chrysler did work out an agreement with Samsung to provide them with auto parts, but it was a very long and expensive way of developing the relationship.

Americans typically get themselves into situations in which they are pitting their reputation and way against the Korean government or against the Korean way of doing things. This is a no-win situation and should be avoided.

Major Problem Areas

The American Chamber of Commerce in Korea (Amcham) identifies a number of specific problem areas for foreign businessmen first approaching Korea that remain despite the two revisions of the Foreign Capital Inducement Law (FCIL) that occurred in 1983 and in 1985.

These revisions liberalized eligibility and approval requirements, and restrictions on remittances of investments were removed. The latest revision includes an approval system designed to simplify and expedite government approval procedures for foreign investments of less than one million dollars and with less than fifty percent ownership in which the participants do not request tax benefits. Investments meeting these guidelines can be approved within ten days if no problems develop.

Amcham notes that one of the negative results of the revision of the investment law is significant reduction in the availability of tax exemptions. It adds, however, that tax benefits can still be obtained in high-tech and export-oriented industries that specifically benefit Korea. Tax exemptions now last for a five-year period, with the foreign investor given the option of taking the tax break during the first five years of a new operation or the next five years.

The problem areas designated by Amcham include the following:

Cooperation and agreement among the various government agencies and ministries concerned is still hard to come by, often resulting in delays in their approval procedures.

Working-level employees in government agencies and ministries do not always approve of policies advocated and announced by senior ministry officials. They have the power to delay or stop completely any application that comes to them, and often do so without any apparent reason for their actions.

There are many "unpublished rules" regarding the government's approval process in any new venture. The applicant too often finds out about these internal guidelines, working rules, and regulations only after applying for approval of a project. Of course, this problem can be greatly reduced if the foreign businessman enlists the advice of attorneys and consultants in Seoul who specialize in dealing with the appropriate government offices.

Lower-level civil servants who are responsible for the administration of the laws governing foreign investment and operation often have little if any international experience, resulting in communication problems, delays, and sometimes serious misunderstandings. The best approach in this situation is to be very patient and helpful, and to maintain a very humble attitude to avoid rubbing the officials the wrong way. Dealing through an experienced troubleshooter who usually already knows the officials and can anticipate their reactions and needs can also, of course, be of significant help.

The protection afforded to proprietary rights in Korea is limited. Patent protection for chemical and pharmaceutical products is so loose that imitators can duplicate a product just by varying the production process slightly. Patent and trademark protection in other areas is more specific but it is still insufficient and generally not strictly enforced.

The monetary value of proprietary technology and rights is not highly developed in Korea, as the above problem indicates. The government in particular, but many companies as well, do not like to pay for technology and often regard return on equity as compensation for proprietary rights. When foreigners insist on being paid royalties for technology, many Koreans feel it is like being asked to pay twice for something.

The remittance of dividends by foreign investors is guar-

anteed under present-day Korean law, but foreign investors whose Korean partners come under special bank regulations sometimes have difficulty remitting profits abroad.

Joint-venture companies wanting to import into Korea
may do so within an officially approved scope of business.
License to import anything other than raw materials for
manufacturing operations is very difficult to obtain.

An unexpected problem, even in Korea, are the extraordinary demands made by the Korean government and numerous associations and charities on foreign companies for
donations. While such donations are ostensibly voluntary,
when the request comes from an official in a powerful
agency or ministry it can be difficult—and may be unwise—to refuse. Here again, a very astute local go-between
who has a wide network of contacts is often needed to
advise the foreign businessman when he can safely ignore
an unreasonable request for a donation.

Amcham members agree that one of the main problems
facing a foreign company wanting to establish a joint-venture operation in Korea is selecting the best possible partner. It used to be that members of the large business/indus-
trial combines called *chaebols* generally made the best joint-
venture partners because of the influence they had with
the appropriate government ministries. Now there are occasions when it can be a handicap instead of a help to join
up with a *chaebol* member because the government's policy
is to favor medium-sized and smaller firms over the giants.

Another, usually surprising, problem in tying up with
one of the more successful Korean corporations is that
making huge profits is still basically regarded as immoral in
the context of Korean values, so any foreign company that
aligns itself with a Korean company that is conspicuous for
its profits is liable to fall victim to some of the opprobrium
felt toward the Korean partner.

Finally, the bigger and more successful the Korean partner, the more likely it is to insist on running the joint
venture its way, regardless of what the foreign partner
thinks is best. This may work fine as long as the policies and
practices of the Korean partner result in the kind of success

the foreign partner is seeking. When it doesn't work out that way, the foreign partner has very little recourse.

Conflicting Goals

Joint-venture operations in Korea are subject to a great many clearly defined cultural strains that put an exceptional burden on the foreign side. One of the most important of these potential problem areas is basic conflict between the goals of the two parties. The primary purpose of the foreign partner is to make a profit and remit dividends outside of Korea. The chief aim of the Korean partner is generally to realize company growth and make an overall contribution to the Korean economy and society at large.

Since both of these positions are virtually absolute, the only sensible recourse is for the foreign partner to be very much aware of this fundamental conflict, discuss it at length during the early stages of the formation of the joint venture, and attempt to reach a mutually acceptable agreement, in writing, on handling this important part of the relationship.

Playing Games with the Books

There is a strong tendency for Korean companies, especially those sponsored by the government, to use "flexible" accounting practices to avoid showing a loss at the end of the year. The main reason for this creative bookkeeping where government-sponsored enterprises are concerned is to prevent the ministry involved from investigating the company and possibly closing it down, replacing the management, or publicly criticizing the management, which would harm the image of the company as well as the individual executives.

When this happens in privately owned companies, it is generally to make the company look in better shape, to save face, and to avoid loss of confidence on the part of suppliers or customers. The foreign businessman looking for an agent or partner in Korea is cautioned to do a thorough financial check before making any final decisions. Otherwise what you see may not be what you get.

Controlling a Joint Venture

An added reason for the foreign company to thoroughly investigate a potential Korean joint-venture partner and to structure the relationship very carefully from the beginning is that eventually (and sometimes much sooner than expected) the foreign partner will most likely lose virtually all influence in managing the venture.

As soon as a JVA is signed, the foreign side loses a significant percentage of its managerial control simply because the Korean side will be primarily responsible for operating the venture and will basically do so as it sees fit. More leverage goes when the foreign partner subscribes to its shares of the stock. There is a third major drop in leverage once the Korean partner has learned all it can or all it wants to from the foreign side. The only leverage that may remain lies in whether or not the Korean partner wants more investment or technology from the foreign company in the future.

The Profit Dilemma

The basic reason that foreign companies go into Korea is to return a profit on their investment and transfer these profits to their home countries or other areas outside of Korea. It is the policy of the ROK government that all profits made in the country should be reinvested in new capital plants to feed the export engine. This policy has been pursued to force-feed the country's export industries and achieve a high annual GNP growth rate, but at the expense of the overall financial stability of the economy. Now saddled with one of the largest foreign debts among the developing nations, Korea's political leaders and government bureaucrats appear to be recognizing that the system they have followed since the end of the Korean War is both unhealthy and dangerous.

About the only foreign companies that have been operating profitably in Korea and have been allowed to repatriate a significant percentage of their profits are firms that are selling services or products that are in high demand by the market and are not available from Korean suppliers.

Foreign companies contemplating investment in Korea should be keenly aware of this aspect of ROK government policy, and take as many measures as possible to avoid getting involved in an untenable situation.

Trademark Protection

It is very important for foreign companies to register pertinent trademarks in Korea prior to establishing a tie-up with a Korean company. The trademarks should be registered separately in the Korean language and the home-country language. It is also vitally important that each of these two registrations show the corresponding registration in the other language.

A Korean trademark does not require prior usage, and is normally issued in about one year. There are numerous specific regulations concerning the registration of foreign patents, so professional help is usually necessary. Among other things, several guarantees of the identity of quality must be provided (by the TAA or JVA, the raw material supplier, etc.) before a foreign trademark can be registered.

Foreign patent holders should also keep in mind that if they allow a Korean to use their registered trademark or if they fail to use it, it may be canceled following a trial brought by someone wanting to break the registration. Koreans frequently register foreign trademarks and then hold them in the hopes of cashing in when the foreign owner opts to enter the Korean market.

Royalties in Process Industries

The Korean government and foreign businessmen have a basic conflict when it comes to the amount of royalties that are proper for the use of patents and technology in the chemical and other process industries. It is the position of the ROK government that such royalties should not exceed three percent, while foreign companies think four or five percent is both fair and needed.

Productivity Korean Style

Foreign businessmen with long experience in Korea say that most purely Korean companies make almost no use of Western management practices in their pursuit of productivity. "The typical Korean company stresses the number of hours worked, without payment for overtime, in its attempts to increase productivity," said one. "There is little or no annual leave, and most efforts are designed simply to get more out of each worker by adding to their working hours, instead of using training programs to increase efficiency."

Korean companies compensate to some extent for this approach to management with their maternalistic treatment of employees, treating them like members of one huge family—which means, however, that as family members they are expected to labor unceasingly for the benefit of the company instead of for themselves, and that they are expected to be satisfied as long as their basic living needs are met.

The attitudes of Korean workers are changing, however, and there is a growing resistance to this method of management. Foreign businessmen are advised to mix their management practices in Korea, making full use of proven techniques to enhance productivity, but at the same time following Korean practices in hiring and paying and in the general treatment of employees.

In all cases, it is imperative that foreign managers in Korea get the understanding and cooperation of their top

Korean managers in implementing any Western-style management practices. Convincing them and lower-ranking employees that "your way" is better can be a long-drawn-out process during which their respect and goodwill are essential.

Marketing Problems

The foreign businessman contemplating a manufacturing operation in Korea normally presumes that one of the primary benefits the Korean side will provide is marketing. "While the situation is changing, the art of marketing products to mass consumers in Korea is still in its infancy," said the resident director of a foreign company in Seoul.

There are exceptions, but generally speaking the foreign company ends up providing most of the marketing expertise for its products in the Korean market. The situation is also complicated by government restrictions on advertising and on importing related items.

Privacy

The concept of privacy within a company is very weak in Korea. Koreans tend to assume that any matter or information that concerns the company also concerns them, and it is difficult to keep anything confidential or limited to the knowledge of an individual. Attempts to keep things from employees of a company are likely to be regarded as distrust or arrogance. This often calls for deft diplomacy in dealing with managers and others on an internal as well as an external basis. It is especially important to avoid appearing unfair to any individual, which includes upsetting his sense of status in relation to his coworkers.

There is generally no problem in protecting company confidentiality as far as outsiders are concerned, and Koreans are very sensitive about their own privacy outside the company.

Working for a Boss, Not a Company

It has often been said of Koreans that, unlike the Japanese, they work for a boss instead of a company. The inference is that Koreans identify themselves intimately with the individuals they work for because it is more natural and easier for them to be loyal to an individual than to a faceless company. This means that the relationship between managers and employees is of vital importance. It also means that the foreign employer or boss in Korea must bear the responsibility of establishing and maintaining a relationship of integrity and trust between himself and his Korean employees.

It is also noted that honor and integrity among Koreans tends to be reserved for those they know, respect, trust, and have an ongoing relationship with. If these conditions do not exist, the same sources say Koreans will readily sign a contract they know they are not going to keep, and will take whatever advantage presents itself.

The Korean View and Use of Contracts

The basic Korean concept of a contract, particularly the view of government bureaucrats, differs fundamentally from the way Westerners view and use contracts. The typical foreign view is that once you negotiate an agreement and sign a contract, that's it; the relationship proceeds forward on mutually acceptable, solid ground. That is not the case at all in Korea. The signing of the contract is usually when trouble begins because from the very beginning the contract is interpreted one way by the Korean side and another way by the foreign side.

Generally speaking, Koreans sign contracts with foreign businessmen to get the relationship started officially. Thereafter everything is subject to change and negotiation. Koreans do not regard the provisions of contracts as written in stone or as the fundamental basis of a business relationship. They regard the personal relationship and the desire for mutual benefits as the foundation of any business arrangement. A contract is essentially nothing more than a symbol of this relationship.

In the context of Korean thought, contractual obligations must change in the same way that business conditions and political situations change, in order for the relationship to be kept current—from their viewpoint, of course.

Being personal agreements rather than immutable laws, the terms of a particular contract go out the door when the signers or the managers of a contract change. From this point, any contract is subject to the interpretations and expectations of the new managers, who devise a new set of unwritten terms to govern the relationship with the second party—and often implement these changes without informing the other side.

This is a vital difference in the concept of a contract that the foreign businessman must understand. The essence is that when a Korean executive signs a contract with a foreign company, he is not necessarily obligating his own corporation to uphold the provisions of that contract. The corporation may not accept the obligation if it has any reason not do so. It may be regarded as a personal matter between the managers who negotiated and signed the contract and the foreign party.

The sanctity of contracts is even less assured where government officials are concerned. Not being direct parties to the agreement, they have no qualms about declaring any contract they do not like as no longer appropriate and needing renegotiation (so as to be more favorable to the Korean side) or null and void, eliminating the responsibility of the Korean party to the contract.

Since government bureaucrats are shifted around regularly, often on an annual basis, contracts between Korean and foreign businessmen are constantly coming up for review by people who know nothing at all about them but who have the power to require that they be altered or scrapped. Incoming bureaucrats frequently feel compelled to demonstrate their efficiency and patriotism by questioning relationships between Korean and foreign companies and ordering significant changes in their contractual arrangements.

Not all the contractual problems between Korean and Western companies is on the Korean side. Western companies frequently play musical chairs with their top personnel in Korea, breaking the personal relationships that foreign managers have established with their Korean counterparts, and making it necessary for their replacements to virtually start over in developing new ties for their companies. If these transitions are not handled thoughtfully and carefully over a period of time (and many of them are not), the switch in personnel gives the Korean side an opening to make unilateral, fundamental changes in the terms of the relationship.

It is especially important for any contract with a Korean company to be as clear, as comprehensive, and yet as flexible as possible. A major challenge is to anticipate changes that are likely to occur that would affect the operation of the agreement, and to make sure they are covered in the contract. Again, a shift in managers involved in implementing a contract can affect its status.

Basically, the contract represents the intentions and understandings of the two participants at the time of signing, and if these are clear and complete, you are off to the best possible start. One problem is making sure that both sides do indeed understand what the other is saying, and are in fact agreeing to that. This may entail a great deal of extra effort in bridging the cultural differences, overcoming communications problems, and really getting down to the "facts." There is always the possibility that both sides will agree to things they really do not like just to get the contract signed, intending to deal with the issue later. This especially applies to the Korean side, and it behooves the foreign participant to make a special, patient effort to draw out the true feelings and intentions of the Korean partners.

The main thing once a contract is signed is to maintain an ongoing dialogue with your Korean counterparts to keep updated on their thinking and to make the adjustments invariably necessary to keep the relationship on an even course. This is often the area in which the Western partner fails, because it requires a conscious commit-

ment—that is time- and energy-consuming (and often cost-
ly)—to adequately nurture the relationship.

Payment Problems

It is common for Korean companies to delay or withhold
payments due to suppliers and contractors for as long as
possible—forever, if the party does not bring enough pressure against them to elicit payment. This happens regularly despite contracts and payment schedules. About the only
way around this problem is to insist on confirmed irrevoca-
ble letters of credit whenever and wherever possible.

When it comes to payment terms, foreign managers are
cautioned to be wary of promises and protestations of financial responsibility, and not to let politeness or naivete
sway them from taking special precautions to ensure
prompt payments when due. I have heard many foreign
businessmen complain after the fact that the Koreans they
were dealing with were so sincere, so frank and forthright
that it was impossible to imagine that they would not live
up to expectations.

Female Employees

The long Korean traditions of men and women virtually
living in separate worlds, in their personal lives as well as
work, is still an important factor in the hiring and use of
female employees. Because of the lingering Confucian attitudes of the past, there is a large and growing pool of well-
educated, talented young Korean women who cannot find
jobs in Korean companies that befit their knowledge and
ambitions.

More and more of these young women are finding employment with foreign companies, where their extraordinary energy, goodwill, and talents are welcomed. Experienced foreign businessmen residents of Korea warn,
however, that using female employees as interpreters or as
representatives when dealing with government officials in

particular, but Korean businessmen in general, can cause
serious problems.

The traditional male attitudes towards women in Korea
are changing at what amounts to a rapid pace, but such
deeply ingrained cultural concepts and customs are impossible to erase in just one or two generations. Foreign businessmen operating in Korea should be aware of this sensitive situation, and restrain their impulse to "force" their
female employees on government officials or others who
strongly resent this change in cultural values and do not
accept it.

While female employees are a valuable asset to a foreign
company in Korea, generally speaking the "face" that the
company presents to the outside must be male to ensure
acceptance and cooperation.

Women and Male Chauvinism

The pressure for Korean wives to have sons took a fright-
ening turn in the 1970s when the amniotic fluid test used
to determine the sex of unborn children was introduced.
Abortions of female fetuses rose dramatically. In 1980 a
more accurate and inexpensive method was introduced,
and the number of abortions went even higher. Mothers-
in-law are said to be responsible for the sex tests and the
decisions for aborting so many female fetuses.

Male chauvinism is still a potent force in the lives of all
Koreans, but Korean women are not passive vassals content to be the playthings of men. Not by any measure.
Virtually every foreigner with any experience in Korea will
tell you that Korean women are stronger than the men,
more clever than the men, more dependable and more
diplomatic (the latter because whatever they do publicly
has to make men look good).

Because of the strong chauvinist character of Korean
males, few Korean women are in management or other
positions of public power. Those few who are in positions
in which they direct males, no matter how low the level of
activity, must be very careful not to upset the ego of the

males. What power females have is more likely to come from a high social position than from an occupational or professional position.

But as women gain more personal economic security and free time, they are going after what they want with extraordinary passion. "They are pulling themselves up by their girdle-straps," said one veteran foreign resident and successful businesswoman in Korea.

7

Barriers Facing Foreign Businessmen

The Great Wall of Korea

There are other specific handicaps in doing business in Korea that derive from traditional attitudes, the fear of excessive foreign influence, and a deep-seated nationalism.

The inferior-superior structure of Korean society, the vertical arrangements in all organizations, and the fact that these arrangements tend to be exclusive and fiercely competitive, make it very difficult or impossible for people in these vertical entities to communicate and cooperate with each other. This often results in irrational and irritating delays in any dealings, particularly those involving the government.

Strong nationalism plays a vital role in the success or failure of foreign companies in Korea. It is most often expressed in a negative way in regard to official government policies. Lower bureaucrats who believe that a stated government policy is bad for Korea (or a Korean company) will go to extraordinary lengths to prevent the policy or the action from being carried out.

Foreign businessmen must learn how to deal with these problems by utilizing a variety of techniques, from enlisting the aid of influential Korean advisors or go-betweens to going to extraordinary lengths to develop close personal relationships in the important ministries and agencies.

Regulation by Competitors

As extraordinary as it might seem, there are several industries in which Korean companies in effect regulate the activities of their foreign competitors. These industries include advertising, banking, insurance, transportation companies, trading companies, engineering companies, and construction companies. Generally, this regulation is effected through industry associations which foreign firms cannot join, or if they can join they are limited to the type of membership that has no power or influence. In the case of the airline industry, however, Korean Air directly regulates the activities of foreign airlines serving Korea.

One of the techniques used by industry associations to control the behavior of foreign competitors is to enact non-tariff barriers that make it difficult or impossible for the foreign firms to do business.

Air Barriers

One of the most significant and conspicuous barriers the ROK has against foreign access to the country involves the airline passenger and cargo business. For years, all matters relating to foreign airlines operating passenger and cargo service in and out of Korea have been under the control of Korean Air, which is theoretically a private company but in effect is an arm of the government.

Everything from the flight schedules of foreign airlines to the handling of cargo has been subject to the official approval of Korean Air. Rental charges and other airport fees have been decided unilaterally by ROK officials. Foreign airlines have not been allowed to have their own warehouses or coordinate air-cargo shipments with any airline except Korean Air.

Materials and supplies used by foreign airlines at Kimpo International Airport and their ticketing offices in Korea are subject to customs duties and long clearance delays. Even such things as inflight magazines, aircraft blankets, baggage tags and tape, and wheelchairs for passenger use are subject to customs duties.

Foreign airlines have been negotiating with the ROK government for years to get the worst of these discriminatory practices eliminated, but so far have had little success, in part because their own governments won't give them sufficient backing.

Tariff Barriers

At this point the Korean government uses a double standard to control and sometimes prevent altogether the importation of foreign products into the country. While adding more and more items to the list of products that may ostensibly be imported without special approval, the government at the same time has raised duties on the products to where their importation is uneconomical, and reserves the right to add an additional surveillance tax on imports that are regarded as disrupting to the market. A complaint by a Korean company, for whatever reason, can be construed as justification for applying this penalty tax.

The surveillance tax regulation also allows the Korean government to reclassify a product as restricted or prohibited if there is any sudden spurt in its importation into the country. The surveillance ordinance therefore reduces the likelihood that an importer will spend a great deal of time and money to develop a market for a particular product, since the more successful he is the more likely the government will block the importation of the item.

The ROK government also uses its discretionary powers to apply other taxes to imported goods, often increasing the actual duties by four or five times the "official" tax rate, thereby effectively barring the products from the country.

Customs Barriers

Discriminatory practices by Korean customs officials are another of the unwritten barriers facing foreign companies exporting to or importing into Korea. These practices range from long delays and additional costs associated with bringing product samples into the country, applying duties when they are not called for (and then denying the opportunity to seek refunds), to the arbitrary re-interpretation of product classifications of items being imported as capital goods and equipment.

Customs officials have or assume the power to use their own judgment in making decisions regarding product classifications, applicable duties, and bonded storage and transportation, and the tendency is for these judgments to favor Korean businessmen and significantly hinder the operations of foreign companies.

This situation is exacerbated by the fact that it is difficult for foreign businessmen to get copies of the applicable customs regulations and standards, so the outsider is often dealing in some degree of darkness.

As usual, the only way to reduce these discriminatory practices, or resolve them once they occur, is to remain outwardly calm and bring into play as many powerful personal connections as possible. It pays to anticipate such problems and engage your Korean network to smooth the way in advance with the appropriate customs officers as well as other government officials.

Association Barriers

Even the Korean Traders Association (KTA), whose primary purpose is supposedly to promote exports from Korea as well as imports and technology acquisition, is used as another means of limiting or prohibiting imports into Korea. Foreign companies may join the KTA as "special members" but so far are unable to derive any significant benefits from the association.

Countertrade Barriers

Government regulations require that foreign companies selling defense equipment and supplies to the armed forces accept countertrade obligations as high as fifty percent or more of the value of each shipment. Other requirements involving the tailoring of products for Korean use sometimes add to the cost of the merchandise. As the American Chamber of Commerce in Korea pointedly notes, the countertrade obligations required by the ROK government are a clear violation of the U.S. Trade Act of 1984.

In virtually every area of trade involving Korea, there is some regulation or practice that discriminates against foreign companies with the specific purpose of denying them fair access. For example, foreign companies operating in Korea may have their own ships and containers, but they cannot operate their own terminals or their own maintenance facilities in Korea. They also cannot open branch offices in Korea or invest in ROK agents in any form—another violation of an ROK–U.S. agreement. Since 1985 the Korean government has also been charging foreign container owners duties on any spare parts bought and used in the country.

Amcham summarizes the situation by noting that, generally speaking, foreign trading companies, wholesalers, and retailers are denied access to Korean markets by a series of highly discriminatory regulations.

Product Classification as a Barrier

The Korean government's classification of products under its CCCN numbering system is also used as a method of controlling or hindering imports into the country. Many products are difficult or impossible to classify precisely under the CCCN system, which leaves the final classification open to the arbitrary judgment of customs officials or other government agencies. Since import duties vary with the classification, this frequently adds to the seriousness of the problem where importers are concerned.

Even more serious, however, is the propensity of customs inspectors to disagree with the previous classification of a product after it arrives in Korea, and either prohibit its clearance or change its classification to one requiring higher duties that price it out of the range of the market.

Advertising Barriers

Under Korean law all broadcast advertising must be placed through the government-owned Korea Broadcast Advertising Corporation (KOBACO). This agency determines all the conditions of television and radio advertising, from commissions to what channels or stations will be used. KOBACO also controls which advertising agencies are allowed to place broadcast advertising by issuing or withholding the appropriate licenses. At present only a handful of the ad agencies in Korea are licensed to engage in broadcast advertising (and their commissions are limited to seven percent for TV ads and eight percent for radio ads).

There are other basic barriers. Foreigners are not permitted to operate ad agencies in the ROK, and foreign ad agencies are not allowed to operate branch offices in the country. Advertising production and the other activities related to creating and placing advertising also are strictly controlled by law.

Despite these restrictions, advertising in Korea is a major industry, and is quite sophisticated. Most of the larger agencies are owned and controlled by major business conglomerates. Several agencies have advisory-type tie-ups with foreign agencies, and are therefore able to provide their clients with some foreign expertise in the domestic market.

8

Adapting to the Korean Business Environment

The Blurring of Morality

The business environment in Korea, a very small country with a large population, is intensely competitive, not only in regard to the best workers and professionals, but also for the allocation of space, licenses, and other factors making up a sophisticated business structure. Since this competitive factor is combined with a very personal approach to business, the whole business environment is susceptible to what international consultant Song-Hyon Jang calls "irregular practices."

Jang says the extraordinary degree of competition and the personal nature of business in Korea has resulted in a mentality in which the end justifies the means, and that the moral implications of much of the business behavior in Korea today are blurred.

It is especially difficult for the newly arrived Western businessman to function effectively in Korea because of the emotional, sensitive, and shifting nature of the business environment. The best possible approach is for the newcomer to enlist the aid of an experienced local consultant and go-between who is a respected and influential part of the business community and can manipulate his way through the maze of personal relationships involved in day-to-day business affairs.

This local representative may be an agent, a joint-venture partner, a broker, or a consultant, but he must be someone in whom the inexperienced foreign businessman can put complete faith to say and do the rights things on his behalf. Otherwise, the results can be disastrous.

Another factor continuously emphasized by such knowledgeable consultants as S. H. Jang is the importance of public image to the foreign company. "Foreign businessmen should give prominent consideration to the public image of their company. Many hurdles can be surmounted if the public relations of a corporation are effective in developing a strong, favorable image," Jang said.

As is so often the case in foreign ventures by American companies, the larger the company the more difficult it seems for it to make adaptations to fit into the Korean political and business environment. One veteran observer said that American bankers in Korea were the most rigid and inflexible of all. "You can recognize them on the street," he said. "Their inflexibility causes them so many problems it is unbelievable, and yet they persist."

Reading Each Other's *Nunch'i*

One of the extraordinary skills the foreign businessman should have to succeed in Korea is the ability to read faces—or to read *nunch'i* (noon-chee), in Korean terms. *Nunch'i* means the look in a person's eyes, the nonverbal reaction of a person to a question, an order, or any interaction with another person. Koreans are very skilled at this subtle art, and take it for granted that others are also.

Dr. C. Paul Dredge, a senior associate of Korean Strategy Associations, writing in *Korea Business World*, recounted a typical incident involving the foreign manager of a joint-venture company in Seoul. The firm's office was located in a very expensive but inconvenient location in Yoido, near the National Assembly Building. The foreign manager found a nice suite of offices in the downtown area of Seoul, less expensive and far more convenient for both employees and visitors.

At the last moment, the Korean president refused to allow the move to take place, and would not explain his reasons to the foreign manager. The situation developed into a sticky impasse that created a great deal of ill will on both sides.

The foreign manager had explained his reasons for wanting to move the office, and believed his rationale had been understood and accepted by his joint-venture partner. He had therefore proceeded in good faith. The Korean president had opposed the move from the beginning, however, and had relied upon the foreigner's ability to read *nunch'i* to understand that he was firmly against the move although he had not said so directly.

The Korean president preferred the Yoido location because it was one of the most prestigious districts in the city. It gave the company "face" on the highest government and business levels, and, as Dredge observed, "The Yoido location had nothing to do with rent and everything to do with where the company president wanted his car to pull up in the morning."

The president and other Korean personnel did not simply come out and tell the foreigner that there was no way they were going to move the offices because they did not want to confront him directly with their objections and cause him to lose face in a contest he could not win. They felt it was up to him to ask the right questions and to "read" the right answers. In the end, as Dredge noted, both sides lost face in a classic case of failure in cross-cultural communications.

Added Dredge: "No amount of training in cross-cultural communication can prepare an expatriate manager to conduct the technical aspects of the business of his company in Korea. But adding cross-cultural sensitivity to his technical and managerial skills and experience puts the manager and his company at a distinct advantage—in discussions of office location, in contract negotiations, in adjustment to family life in Seoul, and in every other aspect of his daily activities, both professional and personal.

"In the past, it has most often been only the Korean businessman who learned the Westerner's ways and made adjustments to accommodate them. The advantages of interculture understanding accrued to him alone. In recent years, however, Korea's position as an emerging economic power has created a flow of economic activity so dynamic that the cultural accommodation of only one side of the Western-Korean partnership is no longer sufficient for either side."

Dr. Dredge says that some expatriate managers have grown tired of hearing that things are done differently in Korea, but "when they and their colleagues put forth the effort necessary to learn the fundamentals of how that is so (or to distinguish between important cultural differences and cases in which citing such differences is little more than a beginning ploy), they can use their knowledge not only to avoid making mistakes, but to gain positive management and negotiating skills."

Social Status

Social status remains a vital factor in personal and business relations in Korea. The foreign businessman who is going to establish an office or factory in Korea must be aware of this and take it into account. To employ a Korean with a low social status as a manager—because of his English-language ability, his experience, or any other qualification—and expect him to be able to effectively manage employees with higher social pedigrees will usually result in problems.

Generally speaking, the higher the Korean is in the managerial hierarchy of a foreign company, the higher his social status should be to avoid undesirable repercussions from other employees.

Social class in Korea is determined by several factors, including ancestry, schools attended, where the individual was born, and where the person presently lives. The social elite in the country is made up of people whose ancestors were high-level government officials, successful businessmen and educators, who were born in Seoul, attended the right high schools and universities (*Kyung Ki High School* and *Seoul National University* are the highest ranking schools in the country), live in a prestigious district of Seoul, and have a relative degree of family affluence.

Rank Has Its Privileges

Koreans have been conditioned for centuries to exist in a hierarchical society divided from top to bottom into carefully prescribed ranks, with each rank having specific kinds of acceptable behavior. This system has been greatly diluted in recent decades but is still of vital importance in the lives of Koreans and to foreigners who do business with Koreans.

There is an upper class, upper-middle class, middle class, and lower class in Korea. In addition to prescribed rules of etiquette within these classes, there is a prescribed form of behavior that is acceptable between the classes.

People in the upper classes generally prefer to avoid direct contact with people who are two or three grades below them or lower, to make sure their own status is not lowered.

Business executives, in particular, are sensitive about their titles and rank, and go to relative extremes to maintain their positions. They take special care not to lower their own status or raise the level of someone below them (by dealing with them on an equal basis).

Foreign businessmen, not being members of Korean society, are normally given the "honorary" status of members of the upper-middle class. Their rank in their company and the rank and image of their company are the next most important factors in their status in Korea. As expected, the higher their titles and the larger and better known their companies, the more prestige they enjoy.

Because of the importance of social position and rank, and the necessity of knowing and following the etiquette that is appropriate for each level, Koreans are obliged to determine these factors as quickly as possible when they meet someone new.

The foreign businessman newly arrived in Korea can

greatly speed up the process of getting acquainted and establishing proper relations with his Korean counterparts, government officials, and others by including his pedigree (important details about the size and sales of his company if it is not well known, the college or university he attended, any upper-class Korean friends or contacts he might have) in his introduction of himself.

The Social Pecking Order

There is a specific pecking order between all Koreans, and until this order is established and recognized there can be very little interaction and no harmony. Every new employee introduced into a Korean group immediately begins steps to find his or her place in the hierarchy. They cannot rest until this is done.

This social pecking order can cause serious problems to the foreign manager who is not aware of it or plays it down. It often happens that the newly arrived Westerner will hire someone for a managerial position simply because he speaks English or has relevant technical knowledge, without considering his educational background or the other things that determine his social position in Korean society. The foreigner then hires other people who have a higher social status to work under this manager. The friction that is likely to result from this situation can seriously affect the operation of the whole company.

Experienced expatriates in Korea avoid this problem by determining the social status of prospective employees themselves, or relying on the input of senior Korean advisors who know how the system works and how to pick the right person for the right job.

The Battle For an Education

There is fierce competition in Korea for entry into the best high schools and universities. Virtually all students in the country take the examinations for Seoul National University, because it is the most prestigious university and a diploma is practically a guarantee of a desirable career in government or business. Unlike Japan's prestigious Tokyo University, which is public, SNU is a government-run school.

Students who fail in their efforts to enter SNU take the results of the examinations to other prominent universities in declining order of their standing, hoping to at least get into one of them. Most of those who fail to get into any university end up settling for one of the junior colleges.

The most prestigious high school in the country, *Kyung Ki,* has been in existence for generations. The most elite of the women's colleges is *Ehwa* (which is sometimes described as the only "real" university for women in Korea).

Just as it has been for the last thousand years, education and schools are of vital importance in establishing the social status of Koreans and determining their careers thereafter. The ties that are established during high school and college days last throughout life and become the network by which individuals conduct most of their private and professional affairs. People constantly scan the newspapers and other media for the names of classmates and alumni as possible business or personal contacts.

Human Harmony in Management

The Korean-Confucian concept of harmony in human relations is expressed in the word *inhwa* (een-whah). It is a concept that incorporates both loyalty on the part of employees and maternalistic concern and behavior on the part of employers toward their workers.

Goldstar Inc. is regarded as the primary advocate of the *inhwah* style of management, and has produced a book by that name that is used as a manual—some say "bible"—by the employees of the company. The guidelines included in the manual include all of the traditional Confucian concepts of loyalty, unselfish goodwill, the maintenance of harmony in all human relations, respect for authority, plus a strong theme of Korean spirit and Korean nationalism based on some five thousand years of historical accomplishments.

When Goldstar established a factory in Huntsville, Alabama, the primary principles of *inhwa* were incorporated into its management philosophy, apparently with significant success.

To Bow Or Not to Bow

Handshaking as a form of greeting and farewell is now an accepted practice in the world of international business in Korea, but it has not replaced the traditional bow. The bow is still the official, formal method of greeting and leave-taking in Korean society, and there are numerous occasions when it is also appropriate behavior for Westerners— such as at formal functions, and when greeting older men and women who have not adopted Western ways.

Whether or not one should shake hands with a Korean is generally not a problem. Koreans are traditionally a friendly, ebullient people and, unlike many Asians, often make the first move to greet a guest or new acquaintance with a good, strong handshake. Like some Latins and Europeans, Koreans will often use both hands when they want to emphasize their goodwill, friendship, or gratitude to someone.

There are several different kinds or grades of Korean bows, depending on the age and rank or social position of the individuals involved as well as on the circumstances of the bowing. The higher the individual, the more shallow his or her bow. Lower-ranking individuals, and those expressing especially deep or sincere thanks, execute deeper bows.

People seeking favors or apologizing bow lower than normal to emphasize the point. Koreans who are used to meeting and working with foreigners generally shake hands instead of bowing.

The bow is not a casual gesture among Koreans. It is a

very direct and conspicuous indication of their relative status, which is jealously guarded, and must therefore be performed properly to avoid giving serious offense.

When Korean businessmen meet for the first time they do not know how to bow to each other until their relative status is established. The first thing they usually do is exchange name-cards. If this is not sufficient to clearly establish a hierarchical relationship, they will quickly inquire about each other's ages, schools, and families.

There is a tendency for foreigners long resident in Korea to subconsciously pick up the habit of bowing, although they generally do not utilize the deep bow. They invariably learn at the same time when it is proper to bow, when a bow can be combined with a handshake, and when to only shake hands. Newcomers who are in doubt about which is appropriate are usually safe if they combine a modest bow with a handshake with everyone except older women who have not been exposed to Westernization. One should bow to them.

Office Calls

Office calls in Korea should be treated as formal affairs, especially if you are visiting a company for the first time. It is not only polite but expeditious to make the appointment well in advance and advise the people you want to see what you want to talk about. Koreans are reluctant to say no directly and do not like to appear uncooperative or unresponsive, with the result that the inexperienced foreign businessman can waste a lot of time making presentations to a company that has absolutely no interest in his idea or project because they may not come out and say so.

One approach is to write the company well in advance, providing as many details as possible about your project, thereby giving the appropriate people in the company time to discuss your proposal and at least make a preliminary decision about whether or not they want to pursue it. Companies with no interest in your project will generally eliminate themselves with a written response or by not responding at all. Another approach—often the best one—is to enlist the aid of a local go-between or consultant who can sound the company out on your behalf.

A significant percentage of all new business relationships in Korea begin with personal connections. The first step in the approach to a company is an attempt to line up these personal contacts. At present, high-level government officials are among the most effective contacts the businessman in Korea can have. If you can get the personal backing of an important ministry official it will open many business doors.

At the same time, Koreans, especially government bureaucrats, generally do not dispense favors without expecting something in return. This something can range from an enhancement of their image to an indirect participation in the venture being proposed. These matters are usually very subtle, and often require the sensitive antennae of an experienced Korean to properly execute—particularly so if you cannot communicate fluently with the official concerned. If you do bring in a local consultant or agent, you have of course added another layer to whatever relationship might develop between you and your target company.

Standing Up At the Right Time

It is common practice for Korean businessmen to indicate respect for visitors to their offices by standing up. It is also regarded as impolite for lower-ranking employees to remain seated while their superior stands. This custom is reinforced by the fact that all young Korean men are required to serve a period of time in the military, where they are drilled in showing proper respect to superiors and guests, including standing up when a superior arrives on the scene.

Higher-level Korean businessmen may not stand up when someone they do not know arrives, and this is particularly so in the case of government officials, unless in-

formed that the visitor outranks them or is a special guest.
Businessmen and government officials may remain seated
if they do not particularly want to see the visitor or do not
like the visitor for any reason.

Until recent decades, women in Korea had virtually no
status and were required to defer to men in virtually all
circumstances. While this has changed considerably, men
still take precedence over women in most common situations where Western chivalry or courtesy would put women
first. Western businessmen who demonstrate unusual
courtesy to Korean women in the presence of un-Western-
ized Korean men may embarrass both the women and the
men. The best idea in this situation is to extend basic courtesy without making a show of it.

In rural areas of Korea, as well as in the most traditional
homes and companies in Seoul and other large cities, wom-
en still take a backseat to men.

Korea's Decision-Making System

The traditional Korean system of decision-making is called
pummi (poom-mee), or "proposal submitted for delibera-
tion." But the system is more form than content, says Dr. Il-
Chung Whang, Dean of Business and Economics College,
Han Yang University. Dr. Whang says the primary use of
the *pummi* system is to diffuse responsibility, and that its use
varies greatly with the size and type of company. Proposals
are written, then circulated vertically within the company.

One of the most important functions of the *pummi* system, according to Dr. Whang, is to provide documentation
for all company programs.

The smaller the company, the less likely it is to depend
on the consensus approach to decision-making. In fact, it is
said that in all of Korea the only company that makes a
concerted effort to follow the consensus approach to management is the huge Daewoo group. According to this view,
the chief executive officer of each of the Daewoo companies expects all decisions to be unanimous, and he sees his
role as asking questions and listening.

The process of decision-making in private industry in Korea is similar to that in American companies that practice participation management. Senior managers have the authority to, and often do, make decisions on their own—especially in the case of founder-owners—but generally speaking, there is a considerable amount of consulting among middle and upper management before major decisions are made.

This process, which is quite different from the well-known Japanese system of "bottom-up" management by consensus, still requires a considerable degree of agreement among all levels of management, and therefore takes time. Foreigners approaching Korean companies cannot confine their dealings to one or two individuals at the top. They must also develop cooperative relationships with all the section or department heads who would be involved in their project.

Despite the surface similarities to Western management, the decision-making process within Korean companies generally cannot be rushed—with the obvious exceptions being in the "one-man" companies run by their founders or their equally strong-minded sons.

The area of decision-making in Korea that stretches the typical Western businessman to the limits (and beyond) is government agencies and government-controlled organizations. Here, the situation is much more like it is in Japan, with a few added twists and turns that often amaze and frustrate foreigners who are not familiar with the psychology and processes that prevail in the ROK government.

Virtually every decision or action wanted from the government or a government-controlled entity must be initiated at or near the lowest level of activity, and then work its way upward through the intricate, sensitive, vertically ranked departments. Because of the paranoia among government employees about being saddled with any kind of individual responsibility, and their obsession about covering every conceivable point, often from every conceivable angle, this process generally requires an inordinate amount of paperwork and redundancy that would try the soul of any but a Korean saint (and they couldn't possibly be immune to all suffering).

Another aspect of interpersonal relations in the structure and psychology of Korean society and business is that there is often very little communication and cooperation between vertically structured departments in a government agency or corporation. This frequently results in the outsider having to deal with different departments as if they were different agencies or companies.

Generally speaking, the Confucian values of Korean society require that all decisions take into consideration the personal feelings and harmony of the group. The manager considering a proposition must give as much thought to its effects on the harmony of the group as to its business or economic benefits to the company. This need for maintaining harmony is sometimes so overpowering that it takes precedence over strictly business considerations. When this happens to the unconditioned Western businessman, he may doubt both the goodwill and intelligence of the Korean businessmen concerned.

This same cultural component of business in Korea colors the entire management process, from the day-to-day flow of work to goal-setting and evaluation. It is an emotional, psychological aspect of business in Korea that the Westerner must understand and deal with effectively to succeed.

In addition to contending with the need for group harmony, the Western businessman in Korea must also beware of expecting any significant degree of creativity from the average Korean manager or worker. The harmony factor prevents a great deal of individual initiative that Westerners normally expect, but equally important in reducing creative thinking in Korea is the rote system of learning used in schools. Not having been encouraged or allowed to think creatively, the average Korean is more likely just to accept things as they are without question.

Western businessmen with extensive experience in Korea add that Korean workers often come up with shortcuts in how to do a particular job, but often without considering the consequences, so that the final results may be undesirable. In such situations, the Westerners add, the typical Korean will say nothing about the problem and it will continue until noticed by someone else.

Negotiation Dos and Don'ts

Koreans are clever, forceful negotiators. They are not conditioned by any sense of fair play, of not taking advantage of a weaker adversary. They will take all they can get. There is also the very strong feeling that foreigners have so much and they have so little that it is only right that they should get more than the foreign side does out of any relationship.

One vital point the foreign businessman should keep in mind when in Korea to negotiate any kind of arrangement is to never let the Korean side know when you are scheduled to leave. If you do, they will invariably lead you on and wait until the last minutes or even seconds to inform you that they cannot accept your terms. This puts the foreign visitor under tremendous pressure to make last-minute concessions in order not to go home empty-handed.

Typically, say old-timers, the visiting American businessman reacts in one of two ways: he "gets hot, blows a gasket, and kills the deal, or he gives in and lets the Koreans have what they want." Japanese businessmen are experienced at this sort of brinkmanship, however, and are usually able to play the game with as much finesse as the Koreans.

A similar approach is often taken in labor-management negotiations, with union leaders assuming seemingly irreconcilable positions until the last few seconds of a deadline, when they will suddenly accept a compromise.

It is essential that the foreign negotiator know his own products and company, know clearly how flexible he can be, and be as knowledgeable as possible about his Korean counterpart. Foreign businessmen often negotiate deals or contracts with Korean companies without leaving their hotels, having only the name and very general information about the Korean side.

Like their Japanese cousins, the Koreans negotiate in groups and are masters at wearing opponents down. The more important the relationship, the more troops the foreign businessman should bring along.

Where the Buck Stops

The top men in Korean companies can be easily identified. In larger companies they are like suns with numerous smaller bodies whirling around them. They are also very conscious and jealous of their position and prerogatives, and can generally be seen personally only by higher-ranking subordinates. Those below a certain level must go through the appropriate channels and be satisfied with dealing only with those slightly above them.

Top Korean executives often make themselves available to foreign visitors, however, primarily out of a sense of hospitality and courtesy because they are foreigners.

Advice for Foreign Managers

Harmonious labor-management relations in Korea require a much larger personal commitment of time and resources than is typical in the average Western company. International business consultant Song-Hyon Jang, president of S. H. Jang and Associates Inc., lists some of the keys to achieving the necessary harmony as multilevel communications, a competitive compensation package, interpersonal company activities, scrupulously fair treatment, and a documented work policy.

Discreet Lines of Communication

"It is particularly important for expatriate managers to open natural but discreet communications channels with their Korean staff, on different levels in all departments," notes Jang. "A deliberate avoidance of bureaucratic protocol will make the head office more accessible to the employees, allowing lines of communication to develop. As long as there is a conscious effort to remove all obstacles and restrictions to a free flow of communication between labor and management, disputes can be prevented or defused. However, in communication with labor, management has to preserve a benevolent but firm and consistent position. Koreans have learned how to respect authority," he adds.

Formula for Keeping Best Workers

Jang says that for the foreign company in Korea to achieve sustained growth and success, it is imperative that it have a competitive compensation scheme, otherwise the company will continuously lose its best workers to other firms with better pay packages. When companies are too small to be competitive in direct compensation, or have budgetary restraints for any reason, Jang recommends such benefits as stock offers, pension plans, unemployment insurance, and health care plans.

Developing Team Spirit

One of the most effective ways to build team spirit and a family-like atmosphere in the foreign company in Korea is to sponsor such activities as picnics, sports activities, a company newsletter or newspaper, recreational clubs, and so on, Jang adds.

Perhaps the most important aspect of managing a Korean work force, however, is to be scrupulously fair to all employees and avoid favoring any particular employee for any reason. "It is sometimes necessary to go beyond the stipulations of labor law," says Jang, "especially in the case where family members of top executives are involved in the business organization."

He adds: "Without compromising standards, the manager's handling of mistakes made by staff members requires a great deal of diplomacy and understanding to prevent them from losing face. To avoid office tension and belligerence, fair, just treatment by the manager is crucial. Proper treatment will tend to weld the loyalty of office personnel to the manager and raise the degree of efficiency and quality of their work."

Jang further notes that it is essential for foreign employ-

ers to put their employment regulations, office procedures, and work rules in writing and have them signed by
all new incoming employees. "Once a complaint is filed by
an employee against company executives, labor authorities
tend to support the employee, so a signed agreement can
save a lot of trouble," Jang added.

Employee Recruitment

Fifty percent of all employee recruitment in Korea is
through informal family and friend connections, which is
most likely to involve people at the lower educational levels. Around thirty-five percent of the remainder is through
"open recruitment"—which refers to direct inquiries by
individuals and those who respond to public announce-
ments about job openings. Only about five percent of employment is provided by school placement programs.

Korea's thirty-six national employment security offices
operated under the supervision of the Labor Ministry, sev-
en public employment services, which are under the supervision of local government, and a number of private agencies provide only about two percent of the work force.

Graduates of technical high schools and vocational training institutes are usually hired through the schools' placement services, and must present skill-test certificates obtained from the National Skill Testing Agency. Graduates
from other high schools must pass company entrance examinations or have the support of a strong connection
within the company. College and university graduates
must pass rigorous examinations that include English-language skill and other subjects studied—as opposed to
knowledge pertaining to work. In some companies, the
presidents themselves participate in the interviewing of
college- and university-level job applicants.

Besides company entrance examination scores, the college or university the individual graduated from, the results of the personal interview, and recommendations from
professors are important factors in who gets hired by the
larger, more successful companies.

Veterans' Law

Because of its system of mandatory military service for all males, the ROK has a Veterans' Administration Law which requires all firms in Korea with twenty or more employees to hire veterans, their spouses, and their children in proportion to the overall number of employees. All foreign companies setting up operations in Korea are subject to this law and must take it into consideration in their hiring practices.

When employers are unable to find their minimum quota of veterans and their family members, the government provides them.

Foreign Workers

Korean companies have few racial or cultural qualms about employing Western workers in their domestic offices and factories. Major employers of foreign talent include Hyundai, Daewoo, and Samsung. Among the hundreds of such employees are engineers, scholars, consultants, and attorneys. This also is reminiscent of Japan in the 1870s and 1880s when thousands of foreign experts were brought in from the U.S. and Europe to help transform Japan's basically agricultural society into an industrialized economy.

Emphasis on Company Training

Larger Korean companies have rigorous procedures for selecting new employees, with each company striving to get the best and brightest of the annual crop of university graduates. The process begins with stiff screening examinations in which the competition may be as high as 100 to 1. Once accepted into a company, an equally rigorous training program begins, lasting from two to five months, and incorporating both "brainwashing" and "survival techniques."

The purpose of the training programs goes beyond just

giving the new employee the necessary knowledge and skills to make a contribution to the company's efforts. They are aimed at molding the newcomers to fit the company's organizational pattern and culture. The training tends to emphasize attitude instead of professional skills, the idea being that dedication, loyalty, and team spirit take precedence over job skill.

These company training programs include intensive courses in foreign languages, particularly English, with the trainees sometimes being sent to university-level language institutes. The companies thus make a long-term investment in their most promising managerial candidates.

Samsung Co., Ltd., founded in 1938 and generally listed as the oldest company in Korea's business history, is famous—or notorious, depending on the source—for its managerial system and its personnel training program, which has been described as "incredibly inhuman." Because of its emphasis on tough training for its employees, the company is frequently referred to as the "Samsung Academy," and is regarded as a training mecca for Korean businessmen.

Samsung's founder, Byung-Chull Lee, who was still going strong in 1987 at the age of seventy-six, carried "report cards" on every executive in the company, and used the cards at the beginning of each new year to decide who was to be promoted or demoted.

Another indication of the dedication of top Korean businessmen to their companies: Daewoo's chairman, Woo-Choong Kim, said he would choose his company over his wife, if it came to a showdown.

Wages, Allowances, and Bonuses

The ROK government suggests guidelines of wages but they are not binding, and most companies ignore them. Foreign companies operating in Korea generally must pay higher wages than their Korean counterparts in order to attract good personnel. One of the expressed reasons for this is that employment in a foreign company is not perceived as permanent, and foreign companies are not expected to follow the same family-oriented maternalistic practices that are typical of Korean firms.

The custom of paying bonuses during the year is an established practice. The amount and frequency of such bonuses varies from industry to industry, but generally amounts to the equivalent of four to six months' salary. Severance pay, based on monthly wages and the number of years worked, is also the practice.

One factor that many foreign managers find upsetting is that Koreans do not consider wage information confidential. Everyone knows what everybody else is getting, and any perception that someone is being overpaid or underpaid becomes a concern of the entire work force. The only recourse is for all wages to be clearly justifiable on the basis of age, rank, schooling, seniority, and any special experience an individual may have.

While work compensation in Korea can be divided into three broad categories of basic wages, allowances, and bonuses, the system varies so much from company to company that it is described by Korean labor authorities as "notorious" for its complexity. They say that no two companies, even in the same industry, have the same wage rate structure.

The Korean system of compensation is also described as being a mix of the Japanese seniority system and the American merit system, distorted by requirements of the Korean Labor Standard Law (LSL).

Basic wages are generally regarded as the most important part of the compensation system, with starting salaries determined by market factors, annual raises determined by length of service and age, along with merit in some companies that have effective evaluation systems. Generally there is also an annual "base up" in wages to account for inflation in the cost of living.

The Korean wage system provides for many kinds of allowances: overtime payment, late-hour working allowance, holiday allowance, monthly rest allowance, annual leave, menstruation and maternity leave allowance—all of which are required by the Labor Standards Law as a minimum. Many firms also provide allowances for special

skills, housing, transportation, large families, perfect atten-
dance, etc.

The LSL requires that workers receive time and a half
for each additional hour worked beyond eight. In many
companies, white-collar workers receive an overtime
allowance of two hours per day as a regular part of their
monthly salary (based, no doubt, on the fact that most of
them unofficially work more than eight hours every day).

Employees required to work between the hours of 10
P.M. and 6 A.M. must be paid one and a half times their basic
salaries. All employers are required to give workers a minimum of one day off, with pay, each week. One day of paid
leave per month is also required by the LSL. These "rest
days" may be accumulated over a year's time for a total of
twelve days. The LSL also requires employers to give workers an additional eight days of leave per year after a year's
service, provided they have not missed any days of work in
the interim; and three days of paid leave if they have not
missed more than ten percent of the working days during
the year.

For each consecutive year of employment, workers get
an additional day of paid leave. Women may take off one
day a month for menstrual leave, and get sixty days off
(with pay) for childbirth.

The bonus system, although not required by law, is well
established in Korea. Companies generally pay bonuses
quarterly, with the amounts varying according to the size
and profitability of the individual company. Sums paid are
usually based on some percentage of the employee's base
monthly wage. Large companies with prestigious public
images sometimes continue to pay high bonuses even when
profits do not warrant such payments.

The Reverse Calculation System

Because of the variety of allowances required by the Labor
Standard Law, Korean companies have developed what is
known in Korean as *Po Kwal Yuck San Jae*, or the "Reverse
Calculation System" (RCS), as a way to simplify the wage

structure. Under this system, the employee agrees to accept a "flat wage" that includes all of the required allowances, but does not require the employer to make all the calculations and adjustments that would be necessary if the many allowances were figured separately each month.

While greatly simplifying the wage system, the RCS nevertheless has its critics who say that it is still so ambiguous that it makes the implementation of such things as retirement pensions, unemployment insurance, and the minimum wage itself very difficult.

The Worker Council Law

In 1980 the Korean government passed a Worker Council Law (WCL) which stipulates that any company with thirty or more employees must organize a Worker Council, with an equal number of workers and managers, to hold ongoing discussion regarding terms of employment and productivity. Wages are a frequent topic of discussion among these Worker Councils. But workers who are members of the councils do not fully represent other workers in the sense of a labor union organization, and are said to be relatively ineffective in achieving wage increases.

Unions in Korea

Korea has both trade unions and enterprise or company unions (the latter similar to those in Japan), all of which come under the Labor Union Law, which greatly limits their activity. Union organization is limited to a few long-established industries, including textiles, and such public enterprises as railway companies, telephone, and electricity (in which striking is not permitted).

ROK unions that are similar to Japanese unions are generally referred to as "company unions," meaning that the union of each company is a distinct, separate organization, made up only of members of that specific company. Some of Korea's unions are known as "Employee Friendship Associations," which is another indication that they differ from regular unions.

The main focus of the current Labor Union Law is to emphasize the enterprise union system over trade unions, primarily as a means of reducing the amount of collusion between labor union leaders and employers in such industries as mining.

Most company unions in Korea are members of local or national federations, which attempt to represent their interests through collective bargaining.

The number of company-union labor disputes in Korea, many of them involving foreign-affiliated firms, has been on the rise since 1984, doubling in 1985. All such disputes are closely monitored by the ROK government, and there are indications that a growing percentage of them are a direct result of deliberate actions taken by so-called student organizers.

There are apparently a combination of reasons why labor problems of one kind or another came to the forefront of labor-management relations in the ROK during the mid-1980s. Among the factors contributing to this development were the appearance of labor organizers, the growing expectations of workers, and the gradual liberalization of the news media—which not only reports on more disputes but tends to encourage them because the participants get more publicity for their cause. The two primary areas of dispute are wages and employee reductions.

There are also "labor brokers" in the building trades in Korea, and it is usually necessary to deal with these brokers in any construction project.

Korea's company unions (common in manufacturing joint ventures and banks as well as other enterprises) concern themselves with work rules and payment provisions, and it is necessary to deal with and stay on good terms with them to have an efficient labor force.

The wage guidelines unofficially set by the ROK government are often more important than the positions taken by unions, because the government monitors them closely and sees that they are followed.

Korea's giant manufacturing and trading combines are

generally not unionized, and there is a consensus that the trade-union movement in Korea has not yet reached the level where it can bring about wage increases that are out of step with productivity.

Unions are far more effective in protecting employment security than in achieving wage increases, and in this there is substantial government backing. Over and above the provisions of the Labor Standard Law, the Korean government discourages employers from laying off workers. To this end, the government maintains a staff of "labor inspectors" who are authorized to monitor the layoff practices of employers, and to bring pressure against them to maintain workers even when there is nothing for them to do.

It is the general feeling among Koreans that it is the social responsibility of employers to maintain the security of workers during bad as well as good times.

Arbitration Taboos

As is typical in Confucian-oriented societies, Koreans abhor the idea of outsiders becoming involved in their business affairs, which they regard as personal. Western-style arbitration is alien to them, is not regarded as a logical or viable choice, and results in a serious loss of face. When Koreans are forced to accept arbitration, the decisions are invariably Korean-style compromises—the kind of solution they prefer to find on their own.

There is a Commercial Arbitration Board in Korea (KCAB), but Amcham records note only one case involving a foreign company in the 1970s. According to the provisions of the Board relating to Korean-foreign disputes, any impaneled board of arbiters will consist of two Koreans and one foreigner and all proceedings will be held only in the Korean language, without provisions for translation.

Amcham's advice is to attempt to get the use of American or ICC arbitration rules in Geneva written into any joint-venture agreement, while noting, however, that the Korean side will strongly oppose the move.

Arbitration procedures under the KCAB are lengthy

and expensive. The first step is usually to give written notice of intent to seek arbitration, which automatically brings into force a ninety-day period when the parties to the dispute are supposed to try to resolve the problem privately. Privately-reached decisions may not be enforceable, however.

If no resolution is reached within the ninety-day period, one of the parties may then file a claim with KCAB. The other party has thirty days to reply to the claim, then the first party has thirty days to respond. If the problem remains unresolved it goes to the Secretariat of the KCAB, which has thirty days to try to settle the dispute by conciliation. If this fails, the problem goes before a board, and drags on for two, three, or more years. Even then one party may refuse to accept any judgment, forcing the matter into a court of law, where the outcome is uncertain to say the least.

The moral, of course, is to avoid the arbitration process in Korea.

9

Summing Up

The Good Side

Despite the many cultural and political handicaps involved in doing business in Korea, there are even more compensations that make the effort worthwhile for a growing number of foreign businessmen. On a personal level, Koreans are a sincere, warm, and friendly people who have often been described as "the Irish of the Orient." They make deep commitments of friendship and loyalty which are permanent if they are treated fairly and with respect. By the same token, if they are mistreated, they make formidable enemies.

It is the personal quality of life and thought in Korea that attracts so many Westerners to persevere in the face of professional and political obstacles. They come to love and admire Koreans and become greatly attached to many aspects of the culture.

In a strictly business context, the ROK represents a large, growing market, with a highly disciplined work force, few labor problems, a high standard of education, an overwhelming ambition to better itself economically and socially, and rapidly rising expectations.

A significant percentage of Korea's top managers were educated in the U.S., and not only speak English well, but are especially friendly toward the United States. There is an urgent need for the kinds of technology, manufacturing, and marketing skills that are available only from the outside, and they are determined to have them. These foreign-educated Koreans in particular are imbued with an extraordinary "can do" spirit that is exciting and catching, and augurs well for this dynamic Asian nation.

Another special advantage that Koreans have, in contrast to the Japanese, for example, is that they feel more at ease with foreigners. Unlike the average Japanese, they do not find associating with or dealing with foreigners such an emotional burden, and are therefore able to deal more effectively with non-Koreans. Japanese businessmen continuously comment on how tiring and nerve-racking it is for them to be in close contact with Westerners, even when they (the Japanese) speak English fairly well. Koreans, on the other hand, seem to thrive on associating with foreigners and are much more aggressive in their relationships.

Koreans are very conscious of their long history and the great achievements of their civilization. This consciousness has been translated into official government policy, which mandates that the cultural heritage of the country be protected and incorporated in the national infrastructure. This concern for and use of art adds a special ambience to life in Korea that is growing more common and significant with each passing year. It adds to the attraction of living and working in Korea, and is a definite plus for the foreign community.

Dos and Don'ts

Every foreign businessman who has spent any significant length of time in Korea has his own list of Dos and Don'ts for doing business in the ROK. Virtually all of these lists begin with: establish a network of strong personal friendships inside and outside of the government, and nurture them carefully and continuously. Almost all actions one takes, personal and business, are fundamentally influenced by one's network of friends.

The government plays such an important role in business in Korea that it is essential to identify the appropriate ministries, agencies, offices, and officials as early as possible and immediately begin the process of developing and massaging that network.

Your commitment to Korea should be long-term, and the man who comes in and sets up the operation, whatever it is, should be prepared to remain in Korea for several years—a minimum of three, and this is cutting it very thin. When transfers are made, it is vital that the replacement be brought in early—like a year or more—to give him time to take over the network of friends and contacts that have been built up. And again, this is not something that can be handled "American style," just by taking the newcomer around, introducing him, and then leaving him on his own. The depth and quality of personal relationships necessary to function effectively in Korea comes only with time.

Patience, good emotional control, a sense of humor, and a long-term perspective are essential for doing well in Korea.

Despite appearances, it is generally unwise to leave important decisions—or in many cases, routine decisions—to the Korean side, even when you are dealing with a very internationalized individual with extensive experience, unless you are willing to accept the consequences of decisions reflecting a strong Korean flavor.

Along the same line, the foreign businessman in Korea cannot leave marketing arrangements up to personal connections, although personal relationships may play a key role in setting up a marketing program.

Other hard-knocks wisdom suggested by veteran businessmen on the scene: don't leave government approval up to a Korean partner; don't locate a JV firm in the same building as your Korean partner; make sure you control (with experienced advice) all hiring and placement.

Newcomer Contacts

The most important contact for any foreign company proposing to do business in or with Korea is the American Chamber of Commerce in Seoul. The Chamber is a strong, vocal advocate on behalf of foreign business, and has accumulated a substantial amount of information and insight on the laws, regulations, and subtleties of doing business in the country.

The experience and insight of hundreds of individuals has been distilled by the Chamber into a publication called "The Business Climate in Korea," which is updated on a regular basis. Among the many Chamber-member committees that contribute to this document are banking, financial services, intellectual property, joint ventures, labor, living and civil affairs, ROK government liaison, taxation and the U.S. Government, trade expansion, and transportation.

Copies of "The Business Climate in Korea" may be ordered from the following address:

The American Chamber of Commerce in Korea
Document Sales Department
Room #307
Westin Chosun Hotel
Seoul 100, Korea

Single copies are $200 each for non–chamber members. To order, send a certified check or money order. Shipping is by second-class mail unless you add an additional amount to the above sum, and specify another class of mail or method of shipping.

The Chamber also publishes numerous position papers on current events that are of special interest and use to businessmen in whatever field, and sponsors briefing meetings for individual companies on a monthly basis, providing newcomers with the insights and guidance of a number of old-timers who have learned the ropes (often the hard way) in years of experience in Korea.

Depending on the kind of business you want to do in or with Korea, the Chamber of Commerce can direct you to other sources of information and help, from the Commercial Section of the U.S. Embassy and branches of foreign banks to appropriate Korean government agencies and offices.

Helpful Organizations

In addition to the American Chamber of Commerce in Seoul, the following offices, agencies, and organizations provide various kinds of useful services and help to foreign businessmen:

U.S. EMBASSY—There are several sections in the American Embassy in Seoul that are set up to assist American business interests. These include the Foreign Commercial Services, the Economic Section, the U.S. Customs, the Science Attache, the Defense Attache, and the Political Section.

Staff members of the Foreign Commercial Services (FCS) section provide counseling on the investment policies of the Korean government and on the specific investment climate, help to identify potential investment partners, and provide financial and other background information on Korean companies. Korean staff members of this section can be especially helpful in elaborating points of interest.

The Economic Section of the embassy offers detailed analyses of the Korean economy in general as well as in specific product or service lines, and offers information and advice on ROK economic policies. The Economic Section, FCS, and other embassy sections also help visiting American businessmen make appropriate contacts within the Korean government.

Other foreign embassies in Seoul have similar services for their own countrymen, of course, but not on the same scale as the U.S. Embassy.

Legal Advice

Law firms are plentiful in Seoul, and many of them have foreign attorneys, including Americans, on their staffs. The legal system in Korea is "totally different" from the U.S. system, so advice from experienced foreign and Korean attorneys can be invaluable, not only in legal matters but in general business matters as well.

Accounting Affairs

Several of the world's top international accounting firms have tie-ups with local accounting firms that allow them to give advice to foreign clientele, and there are local firms that are themselves highly respected in the foreign community. In addition to matters concerning bookkeeping, taxation, and auditing, these companies are also involved in executive placement and consulting on a wide range of subjects involving business in Korea.

Cost of Living

Statistics compiled by Amcham show that Korea, particularly Seoul, is one of the most expensive countries in the world for expatriate businessmen and their families. Rental housing, food, private transportation, schools—all are far more expensive than anywhere except perhaps Japan.

Each year Amcham publishes an "Expatriate Cost of Living Survey" that covers housing rental costs, utilities, domestic help, private transportation, and schooling. The Chamber also publishes a periodically updated book entitled "Living in Korea," which includes a wealth of information on all the key areas of living in the ROK.

The Head-Office Syndrome

There comes a time in the life of most businessmen stationed abroad when the cultural, legal, and other problems they face in their foreign post are surpassed by problems with their own head offices. These problems result from a combination of many factors: the home office wants something done in hours or days that actually takes weeks to accomplish; the HO sends over requests or instructions that are impossible to follow because of cultural, political, or other reasons; HO visitors get the impression that their expatriate managers spend most of their time in the bars and restaurants of first-class hotels; and so on.

This syndrome is especially strong in many companies with operations in Korea, in part because when their ranking executives visit Seoul the red carpet is rolled out for them and they are inundated with typical Korean hospitality. To them, Koreans are the friendliest, most solicitous, generous, and accommodating people in the world, and working with them has to be one long joyride.

Expatriate managers who are burdened with this breed of top management end up spending an inordinate amount of their time trying to explain why things cannot be done the way some vice president ten thousand miles away thinks they should be done, and trying to get decisions or some other kind of action out of the home office.

Recommended Reading Materials

A Handbook of Korea, Korean Overseas Information Service, Sam Hwa Printing.

Government Business and Entrepreneurship in Economic Development: The Korean Case, by Leroy John and Sakong Il, Harvard University Press.

Industry in Korea, Korea Development Bank.

Investment Guide to Korea, Korea Chamber of Commerce and Industry.

Joint Ventures in Korea: Corporate Guide to Opportunities and Problem Solving, Business International, New York.

Korea—Problems and Issues in a Rapidly Growing Economy, by Parvez Hasan, Johns Hopkins University Press.

Living in Korea, American Chamber of Commerce in Korea, Seoul.

Republic of Korea: A Guide for Businessmen and Investors, Small Accounting Corporation.

A number of excellent general-interest books on Korean history, culture, lifestyles, sightseeing, etc., are available from bookstores. Among them: *Korea—Beyond the Hills,* by

H. Edward Kim; *Korean-Insight Guides,* by APA Productions of Hong Kong; *Korean Patterns,* by Paul Crane; and *Through a Rain-Spattered Window,* by Michael J. Daniels.

Miscellaneous

Folklore Day

Businessmen traveling to Korea should keep in mind that the country is pretty much locked up for three to five days over the lunar New Year, which is now officially called *Minsok Jol* or Folklore Day. Most older Koreans try to visit their birthplaces over this period, which means that all transportation systems in and out of major cities are jammed. If you plan on traveling in-country during this national holiday, reservations should be made several weeks in advance, and confirmed several times.

Many Korean companies charter buses to transport employees to their hometowns for this important holiday period—which begins at the end of January or in early February, and lasts for three to five days.

Most Koreans also celebrate New Year's according to the Western calendar, taking off from one to three days at the beginning of January.

Sharing Taxis

The demand for public transportation is so great that *hapsung* (hop-sung) or "taxi sharing," which developed in the 1950s, is still common in Korea. During busy periods, drivers pick up as many as three passengers who are going in the same general direction, dropping them off one by one at their destinations.

Avoiding Visa Problems

Under current Korean laws, there are eighteen classes of visas issued by the Immigration Bureau of the Ministry of Justice (MOJ). As usual, applications for visas to enter Korea must be made outside the country at Korean consulates or embassies. These applications are then physically sent to the MOJ in Seoul for review and approval.

For any visa other than tourist, the MOJ usually requires copies of a work contract covering the conditions and terms under which the individual will be employed in Korea, a letter from the employer certifying the need for the foreigner's particular skill and the employment terms, along with guarantee letters and a document certifying that the foreigner will leave Korea when the contract ends.

This process can take several weeks to months, so it is advisable to start the proceedings well in advance of an expected departure date. Other points to keep in mind:

Once a visa is issued, it cannot be changed in Korea. The holder must leave the country and reapply at an overseas consulate or embassy. The status of a visa also cannot be changed in Korea. A foreigner resident in Korea for more than sixty days during one year may become subject to Korean income taxes.

Those contemplating teaching English in Korea should be aware that visas may not be granted unless the school concerned is recognized and licensed by the government.

VISA CATEGORIES
9-1   Diplomats
9-2   Public affairs personnel
9-3   Treaties/Agreements negotiators, staff
9-4   Tourists, conventioneers, athletes, artists, short-term trainees
9-5   Journalists
9-6   Clergymen
9-7   Technicians
9-8   Commercial (businessmen assigned to Korea by a foreign company)
9-9   Commercial (businessmen working in joint-venture firms)
9-10 Educators, teachers
9-11 Employee of Korean company
9-12 Student
9-13 Trainee (long-term)
9-14 Entertainer, performer, athlete
9-15 Dependent of resident in Korea

9-16 Permanent resident
9-17 Accompanying foreign entrant (who has appropriate visa)
9-18 Miscellaneous

Korean Universities

Universities in Seoul
Seoul National University
Yonsei University
Korea University
Sungkyunkwan University
Dongkuk University
Hanyang University
Kyung Hee University
Choong Ang University
Seo Kang University
Hankuk University of Foreign Studies
Kunkuk University
Dankuk University

Women's Universities in Seoul
Ehwa Women's University
Sook Myung Women's University
Soo Doo Women's Teachers' College

Other Universities in Korea
Pusan National University
Dong A University of Pusan
National Universities in the provinces

Job Titles and Their Korean Equivalents

Foreign	Korean	Translation
Chairman, Board of Directors	Hwoe Jang	(Chairman of the Board)

President	Sa Jang	
Vice President	Boo-Sa Jang	
Managing Director	Chunmoo Ee-Sa	(Principal Director)
Director	Sangmoo Ee-Sa	(Standing Director)
General Manager	(no equivalent)	
Department Manager	Boo Jang	(Department Chief)
Assistant Department Manager	Cha Jang	(Vice Department Chief)
Section Manager	Kwa Jang	(Section Chief)
Assistant Section Chief	Kye Jang	(Branch Chief)
Senior Clerk	Joo Im	(Principal Job)
Clerk	Kye Won	(Branch Member)
Typist	Ta Jasoo	
Messenger	Sa Hwan	

Factory Titles

Factory Manager	Kong Jang Jang	(Factory Chief)
Department Manager	Boo Jang	(Department Chief)
Section Manager	Kwa Jang	(Section Chief)
Supervisor	Kye Jang	(Branch Chief)
Foreman	Joo Im	(Person in Charge)

Other Titles

Secretary	Bee Seo	
Bookkeeper	Kijangsuki	
Driver	Oonjunsoo	

Department Names

Accounting	Iiwegae
Engineering	Engineer
General Affairs	Chong Mu
Machine Shop	Keekyea Kong
Materials	Chache
Material Control	Chache Kwan-ree
Plant Maintenance	Kong Jang Sisol Kwanree
Production	Saengsan
Quality Control	Pumcheel Kwanree
Sales	Panmae
Shipping/Receiving	Balsong/Sunap

Business Hours

Government offices are open from 9 A.M. to 6 P.M. on weekdays from March through October, and from 9 A.M. to 5 P.M. from November through February. Most business offices are open from 8:30 A.M. to around 7 P.M., generally six days a week. On Saturdays government offices are open from 9 A.M. to 1 P.M.; banks from 9:30 A.M. to 1:30 P.M.

Currency

The unit of Korean currency is the *won*, which comes in W500, W1,000, W5,000, and W10,000 notes, and W1, W5, W10, W50, W100, and W500 coins. Visitors to Korea may bring in up to US$5,000 without declaration. Sums over this amount must be declared on a "Foreign Exchange Record" form.

The *won* exchange rate fluctuates. Bank notes and travelers checks can be converted into *won* at exchange banks and authorized money exchangers (which includes all international hotels).

When visitors depart from Korea they may reconvert all unused *won* to U.S. dollars when accompanied by a receipt of foreign currency conversion. When no conversion receipt is available, the maximum that can be reconverted is US$500.

Foreign currencies can be taken out of the country up to the amount imported and declared. Only W500,000 can be imported or exported at any one time.

Credit Cards

Most international credit cards, including American Express, Carte Blanche, Diners Club, Master Charge and Visa, are accepted at leading hotels, department stores, and restaurants as well as by many visitor-oriented shops in the major cities. The most commonly used local credit cards include BC (which is affiliated with Master Charge), Citizen's National Bank (local and Master), Segong (KOCA card), Korea Exchange Bank (Visa), and Korean Express.

Tipping

Individual tipping (to taxi drivers, at restaurants, etc.) is not the practice in Korea. The most common exceptions are to porters at transportation terminals, to guides who do an exceptionally good job, and to taxi drivers who go out of their way to aid passengers (with their baggage or finding addresses).

In lieu of tipping, however, most hotels, restaurants, and tourist shops add a ten percent service charge and a ten percent tax (Value Added Tax or VAT) to their bills, which of course adds a total of twenty percent to the cost of many goods and services.

Newspapers and Magazines

There are two English-language newspapers in Seoul, the *Korea Herald* and the *Korea Times*, both of which are published daily except Mondays. A weekly news magazine, *Korea News Review*, provides summaries of major news and upcoming events.

There are also two monthly English-language business

magazines that cover the Korean scene, *Business Korea* and *Korea Business World*. Both provide a substantial amount of information and insights that are valuable to foreign businessmen.

Subscription rates and ordering addresses are:

Business Korea, Yuido P.O. Box 273, Seoul 150, Korea
    North and South America, 1 year, US$60
    Europe and Africa, 1 year, US$65
    Asia and Oceania, 1 year, US$55
    Within Korea, 1 year, US$40

Korea Business World
    Suite 303 Shinsong Bldg.
    25-4 Yoido-dong, Yongdungpo-gu
    Seoul, Korea
    Mailing address:
    Yoido P.O. Box 720, Seoul 150, Korea
    North & South America US$60
    Asia & Oceania US$55
    Europe & Africa US$65

Korea Trading Post is a biweekly bulletin published by the Korean Traders Association (KTA), covering Korean industry and products. It is free for the asking. CPO Box 1117, Seoul, Korea. Fax: (02) 754-13307.

Leading news magazines from the U.S. and Asia are available at hotel newsstands and many bookstores.

Telephone Service

Public telephones for local calls are readily available in office buildings and sidewalk booths in major Korean cities. A three-minute local call, on a red or green telephone, costs W20 (two 10-won coins). The connection is broken automatically after a ten-second warning signal, unless additional coins are inserted.

Public phones for long-distance calls are yellow in color, and are located in major hotels and at post offices.

Emergency Phone Numbers

To call the police, dial 112. To report a fire, call 119. If you need medical assistance, contact your hotel telephone operator, the police (there are police boxes on many street corners), or ask for assistance from people in shops, stores, or restaurants, or from security guards at office buildings.

Air-Raid Drills

At this writing, the ROK continues to conduct regular air-raid drills, usually on the fifteenth of each month. The dates of the drills are subject to change, however, and are announced the day before in local newspapers.

The drills last twenty to thirty minutes, during which time all traffic is required to stop and all business activity ceases. People outside may be requested to enter lower-level shelters.

Airport Tax

All passengers departing from Korea are required to pay an airport tax of W3,700.

10

Glossary

Achom (ah-choam)—It is very important in Korea to maintain a positive, friendly demeanor and avoid hurting anyone's feelings. Part of this process consists of the generous use of compliments and flattery, or *achom*. Foreigners not familiar with the social custom are likely to confuse such flattery and compliments with extraordinary politeness, and a friendly, easygoing, cooperative attitude. While the latter may be true on an individual basis, the practice of *achom* has a far more serious purpose. See *kibun*.

Amukuto anida (ah-muu-kuu-toe ah-nee-dah)—This is a common response when someone in Korea is given a hard task. It means "It's nothing. I can do it easily," and is indicative of the "can do" spirit of Koreans.

Apatu (ah-pah-tuu)—The size and location of an *apatu* (apartment) is of special importance in Korea because it is associated with social class, which in turn is an important factor in the type of work one is able to obtain and where one works. Foreign managers in Korea should be aware of the class factor and take it into account in their dealings and relationships with Korean employees.

Baek ji wiim (bake jee weem)—Literally "trusting in white paper," this term is often used to infer that someone is doing business on the basis of nothing more solid or permanent than a piece of paper with a signature on it—

which is a pretty good description of a contract. The concept derives from the fact that Koreans believe a deep personal relationship is the only proper foundation for a business relationship.

Bal i nulba (bahl ee nule-bah)—The person in Korea who seems to know everybody and be able to do almost anything through his connections is said to have a *bal i nulba,* or "wide leg," instead of a "wide face" as in Japan. Because most business within private industry as well as with the government is based on having extensive personal contacts, the person with a "wide leg" is especially valued in Korea.

Bangsuk ul galda (bahng-suuk ule gall-dah)—This literally means "to put a cushion under someone" (to make sitting more comfortable). It is used in reference to wining, dining and otherwise catering to a person you want something from—at which Koreans have a special talent.

Bokshin (boak-sheen)—*Bokshin* refers to an aide or assistant who is so trusted by the boss that he is allowed to act on his behalf. The literal meaning of the term is, roughly, "man in his belly."

Bottle-keep (boe-tahl-kee-puu)—The practice of keeping one's own bottle at a favorite bar has been introduced into Korea from Japan, but it is not common. "We drink so much there is almost never anything left in a bottle to leave at a bar," said a Korean executive, laughing.

Bural an chok (buu-rahl ahn choak)—A man who builds up a business enterprise with hard work but little capital is said to have done it *bural an chok,* or "only with balls."

Bu sajang (buu sah-jang)—This is the Korean term for "vice president." It may also be used as "department head" or "division head."

Byul jang (buul jahng)—Literally a "remote house," this is the Korean word for a recreational villa, usually on the coast or in the mountains. Many of the *byul jang* in Korea are maintained by the larger companies for their employees.

Chaebol (chay-bowl)—This is the term used in reference to Korea's huge business-industrial complexes such as Daewoo, Lucky-Goldstar, Sunkyong, Sangyong, and Samsung. It is the Korean equivalent of the Japanese term *zaibatsu*.

Chagayong unjonsa (chah-gah-yong uun-joan-sah)—Just as in other countries, personal chauffeurs (*chagayong unjonsa*) are a highly prized status symbol in Korea. They are especially practical for businessmen who work in the downtown areas of Seoul and other major Korean cities because of the scarcity of parking places.

Chansa (chahn-sah)—As part of their concern for face and feelings, Koreans make great use of compliments (*chansa*), but the custom is chauvinistic in that men do not customarily compliment women. It is advisable for foreign men in Korea to be aware of this taboo when they are tempted to conspicuously praise the looks, dress, or accomplishments of Korean women in the presence of Korean men.

Chehan (chay-hahn)—This is the word for "restriction," which is often used in Korea, particularly in relation to imports and exports.

Chibaein (chee-by-een)—Koreans take such titles as *chibaein* (manager) very seriously, and it is common to address them by their titles instead of by their names, particularly since so many people have the same family name (in a company with one hundred employees, as many as ten or more may be named Lee, another ten or so may be named Pak, and there may be ten or more Kims, etc.).

Chido (chee-doe)—This is the Korean equivalent of the Japanese term *shido*, which is used in connection with government "guidance" of industry. It is somewhat less commonly used in Korea because there is very little effort to disguise or deny that the government's role is more in the nature of control than guidance.

Chim shin uro (cheem sheen uu-roe)—The Korean term for "pure heart," this is used in reference to a person of impeccable integrity and sincerity who can be depended upon to do what is right. It is a quality Korean employers pay special attention to in their hiring practices.

Chinchok (cheen-choke)—Korea's strong family orientation extends well beyond the nuclear family to include relatives (*chinchok*) two, three, and four times removed. This sometimes complicates their relationships with Westerners. The foreigner who marries a Korean is often surprised at the size of the "family" he or she has acquired (and is obligated to in many ways).

Chip an (cheep ahn)—The Korean equivalent of the Japanese *uchi,* which is used in the sense of "my house," "my home," "my company." *Chip an* literally means "inside the house" and is used in the same way as the Japanese word. The usage indicates the close relationship Koreans develop with their place of employment, putting it on the level of their home.

Chisongnyok (chee-song-nyoke)—This is the term used by Koreans in reference to their incredible capacity to endure physical as well as mental hardships. It is seen as one of their major national strengths.

Chohoe (choe-hay)—The "morning meeting" or "morning ceremony" (*chohoe*) has been adopted by most major Korean companies, and the practice is growing. The *chohoe* held by some companies is very ceremonial; in some, the national anthem is played.

Chonmae (chone-my)—The Korean government operates a number of monopolies (*chonmae*) as a method of earning income. The monopolized products include ginseng and tobacco.

Chongchi (chong-chee)—Politics (*chongchi*) plays some role in almost every foreign business deal consummated in Korea, so this is a useful word to know. Another important word is *chongbu,* meaning "government."

Chong ddae (chong-dday)—Literally "the barrel of a gun," this is the Korean version of "hired gun," or someone who does an unpleasant job for the boss.

Chongui (chong-we)—The Korean concept of justice (*chongui*) is based more on what is good for society and the country than on what is best for the individual. Because of this philosophical difference, foreigners who become involved in court cases in Korea are often disappointed with the outcome.

Chongyong (chone-gyong)—Because of the vertical structure of their society and the importance of maintaining and protecting one's social status, Koreans are very sensitive about paying and being paid proper respect (*chongyong*). Foreigners living and working in Korea must learn something about this etiquette and make use of it in order to function effectively.

Chon jimina (choan jee-me-nah)—This translates, more or less, as "one centimeter of feelings," and refers to the small gifts that Korean businessmen customarily give to people they meet during the course of a trip, to show appreciation and express thanks for relatively small favors. It is a good practice for foreign businessmen to emulate on their trips to Korea.

Chonmae tuko (chone-my tuu-kah)—In Korea, foreign patents (*chonmae tuko*) must be registered in both Korean and the language of the originating country.

Chonmun-ga (chone-muun-gah)—While the idea of paying a consulting fee or a royalty to someone for their advice or the use of their intellectual achievements is basically foreign to Koreans, they still recognize the value of *chonmun-ga,* or "experts," and make use of a growing number of foreign consultants, engineers, and scientists.

Chuchon (chuu-chone)—A *chuchon,* or "recommendation," is very important in making new contacts in Korea. The recommendation may be written or verbal. The best is verbal and in person.

Chukcheil (chuke-chay-eel)—Folk festivals (*chukcheil*), many of them dating before recorded history and shamanistic in origin, continue to play a vital role in the lives of most Koreans. They are especially important events in rural areas.

Chulhyong sawon (chule-hyong sah-woan)—This is a "worker or employee on loan" to an affiliated or subsidiary firm. It generally carries the connotation that it is a temporary situation, but the transfer may also be permanent. Valued employees are often sent out to help rescue smaller affiliated companies that have gotten into trouble. It is also a common practice when one company acquires another firm, either to control it or to assist its management.

Chungjae (chung-jie)—Koreans abhor the idea of *chungjae,* or "arbitration by outsiders," and go to extreme lengths to avoid it. They regard such a move by company executives as a public admission of their incompetency and general unfitness to direct a company's affairs. But "mediation" between the parties involved, which is the same word in Korean, is the accepted method of resolving disputes. The experienced mediator (*chungjaein*) is therefore an important person in Korean society. The same word also means "middleman" and "intermediary."

Chusik hoesa (chuu-sheek hoe-eh-sah)—A "stock company." The most common type of company organization in Korea.

Daedulpo (day-duul-poe)—Literally "stone and pillar." Figuratively, the person in an office, agency, or company who is primarily responsible for keeping it going and for its success. "Stone" refers to a foundation stone, and "pillar" to what holds a building up. The "backbone" of the company.

Daepochip (day-poe-cheep)—This is the Korean equivalent of the Japanese word *akachin* (ah-kah-cheen) or red lantern, symbolic of drinking and drinking establishments. However, the literal meaning of *daepochip* is something like "house of artillery" or a place where big guns are kept. The inference is that when people drink they often shoot off their mouths. The more they drink, the bigger become the "shots" they fire. Red lanterns are not hung in front of Korean drinking places, as they are in Japan.

Dollah box (dollar box)—A company's most profitable product, line, or department is frequently referred to as its "dollar box." A company's source of financing may also be called its "dollar box."

Dong chang saeng   (dong chahng sang)—A Korean businessman's biggest asset is his *dong chang saeng,* or "network," made up of classmates, alumni brothers, friends made in the military, relatives, relations by marriage, and other close friends he has made along the way. The foreign businessman in Korea must take the same approach, developing his own network.

Danyom hada   (dahn-yoam hah-dah)—This is the Korean equivalent of "throwing in the towel" or giving up or dropping something, such as negotiations that are not going anywhere or a product that is losing money. The literal translation is something like "cutting one's mind."

Dulinda   (duu-leen-dah)—This is a commonly used greeting among businessmen in Korea when they make courtesy calls on customers or contacts. It means, more or less, "Are you at peace?" in reference to the fact that Korea has experienced so much warfare in its history. The present-day meaning is something like, "Are things going well?"

Ggara mungeida   (gah-rah muun-gay-dah)—Literally "to crush with one's rear end," this is the equivalent of killing a proposal or application by sitting on it, something that government bureaucrats in Korea and elsewhere are often accused of.

Haengjong   (hang-joang)—While generally following Confucian principles, the *haengjong,* or "administration," in Korean companies is often significantly affected by the personal style of the president or chairman, and when several members of the same family are involved in top management.

Haengjung chido   (hang-juung chee-doe)—This term refers to the "administrative guidance" the Korean government exercises over virtually all areas and categories of business. The "guidance" is based on the power inherent in the government's control of licenses, import and export quotas, taxation, etc., rather than specific laws.

Hachong   (hah-chong)—All of Korea's large, well-known companies have a network of *hachong* (subcontract firms) beneath them. Just as in Japan and other countries, the subcontract firms are used as cushions to shield the major companies from fluctuations in demand, prices, and exchange rates.

Hahn (hahn)—A very important word in the story of modern-day Korea, *hahn* refers to all the human yearnings—physical, social, political, emotional, intellectual, and spiritual—that were suppressed by their Confucian-oriented feudalistic government for more than five hundred years. Koreans say the extraordinary energy, dedication, and sacrifices that were responsible for much of the economic miracle they achieved during the 1960s and 1970s flowed from the release of the pent-up psychic force of *hahn*.

Hakuksang (hah-kuuk-sahng)—In Korea's tightly structured vertical society, *hakuksang,* or "going over a superior's head," is a very serious matter. Management ranks in larger companies are as clearly defined and as guarded as those in the military.

Hangugo (hahn-guu-go)—The Korean language.

Hanguk (hahn-gook)—This is the Korean word for Korea. It means "Great Country." The word for Korean person is *Hangug-in* (hahn-goog-een).

Hanguk umshik (hahn-gook uum-sheek) or **Hanshik** (hahn-sheek)—This is the term for "Korean food," which the visitor will find very useful. If you don't want to eat Korean food every day, it is also advisable to learn how to say *yang shik* (foreign food).

Hangul (hahn-guul)—The Korean system of writing—the special phonetic characters used to write the language—was developed by a team of scholars in the early 1400s at the request of King Sejong. It is the only writing system known to have been deliberately designed by a group of experts over a short period of time. The symbols can be learned in a day or so, as opposed to the many months or years required to learn the ideograms used in Japan and China, and to a lesser and decreasing degree in Korea.

Hanjan hapshida (hahn-jahn hop-she-dah)—A commonly heard term in Korea's business world, this is the equivalent of "let's have a drink." It is rare, however, for the guest to get by with having only one drink. Korean businessmen tend to put as much enthusiasm and energy into drinking as they do working.

Han jan man (hahn jahn mahn)—*Han jan man,* or "only one glass," is the common Korean invitation used to invite someone out for a drink and a talk, usually after business hours. "One glass" should not be taken literally.

Hapcha Hoesa (hop-chah hoe-eh-sah)—A limited partnership company.

Hapmyng Hoesa (Hop-ming hoe-eh-sah)—A partnership company, a form of company organization that is rare in Korea.

Hoegyesa (Hoag-yay-sah)—The *hoegyesa,* or accountant, in a Korean firm is an important individual. It can be very helpful for the foreign businessman to establish a strong personal relationship with the *hoegyesa.*

Huisaeng ta (hwe-sang tah)—Literally a "sacrifice batter," this is a person sent in to learn as much as possible before serious negotiations start, or used some other way as a front man who plays a limited role to gain a fast advantage.

Hukmak (huke-mahk)—It is common in Korea for an individual behind the scenes (*hukmak*) to be the one who really exercises power. *Hukmak* means "black curtain." Another term also used is *makhu shil yokja* (mahk-huu sheel yoak-jah), which means "strong man behind a curtain."

Hwandae (hwahn-die)—This is the word for Korea's famous hospitality, which can be overwhelming, but pays off in the goodwill and cooperation that it generates.

Hwanyong hoe (whan-yong hay)—Koreans are noted for their elaborate *hwanyong hoe,* or "welcoming receptions," which are part of their custom of conspicuous hospitality. They are customary when welcoming new employees into a company, and when formally greeting newly arrived guests, especially from abroad.

Hyongshikchogin (h'yong-sheek-choe-gheen)—Korean businessmen and government officials tend to be *hyongshik-chogin* (formal) in their behavior, especially toward foreign guests.

Hyopoe (hyahp-po-eh)—Associations (*hyopoe*) are a vital aspect of business as well as personal affairs in Korea. Generally speaking, many of the associations having to do with business constitute obstacles to foreign companies dealing with Korea, since they are exclusive and are designed to give the Korean members an advantage over foreign companies.

Ilbonsaram (eel-bone-sah-rahm)—This word means Japanese (person), and is something Koreans do not like to be mistaken for. Generally speaking, Korean men are physically larger and more muscular than Japanese, and the women are taller and have larger busts and wider hips than their Japanese counterparts.

Ilbulrae (eel-buul-ray)—"Working like an insect" is the Korean equivalent of a workaholic. The term is used often, generally in a positive, complimentary way. As one man said, "In Korea, the person who works like a bee is respected."

Inhwa (inn-whah)—One of the key principles of traditional Korean society, *inhwa* means "harmony," in this case, based on Confucian concepts of hierarchical relationships between people, respect for elders, obedience to authority, coordinated group behavior, and decisions by consensus.

In maek (inn make)—These are the personal connections that are so essential to both private and business life in Korea. Instead of going from the objective to the subjective, as in common in the West, virtually all Korean relations start with the subjective or personal side. The importance of these personal connections is suggested by the term *in maek*, which means something like "human pulse."

Ipto ssagi (eep-toe sah-ghee)—This refers to the practice of hiring high school or university students before they graduate, in order to get the pick of the "crop." The word literally means "standing rice," and originally referred to brokers buying rice before it was harvested. It is also used in reference to buying stocks or merchandise before it is made or while it is still in the factory.

Insa (inn-sah)—The *insa*, or greeting, plays a special role in social and business affairs in Korea, because it establishes the relative social position and rank of the individuals concerned, and reaffirms personal relations. Businessmen regularly visit their key contacts to greet them formally as a way of sustaining their network of connections. A written greeting is an *insa jang*.

Insa idong (een-sah ee-dong)—Large Korean companies systematically rotate employees from department to department and branch to branch in early spring, as part of their overall on-the-job training. This system, known as *insa idong*, contributes to the long-term efficiency and value of employees in many ways, but for outsiders dealing with individual companies it means they are faced each year with making new contacts and dealing with a new set of personalities.

Jaebul (jay-buul)—Many companies in Korea belong to a specific *jaebul*, or group, and in various ways coordinate their operations with the leading firms heading up their groups. *Jaebul* is also used in reference to financial groups.

Jajunggu bakwi dolligi (jah-juung-guu bahk-we dole-lee-ghee)—A person who is being given the runaround by a company or government agency is said to be *jajunggu bakwi dolligi* or "pedaling a stationary bike." In other words, he isn't going anywhere.

Jal butak hamnida (jahl buu-tock hahm-nee-dah)—One of the most used phrases in the Korean language, this means something like "please do whatever you can for me." It is said to someone when you want them to take care of something or do something, whether it is a favor or something they are obligated to do anyway. It is an institutionalized, stock phrase, and is the equivalent of Japan's *yoroshiku onegaishimasu*. It is used in both informal and formal situations, and is a way of humbling yourself so the other person won't regard your request as arrogant.

Jang ki (jahng kee)—Koreans take great pride in their ability to sing or perform some other kind of entertaining skill, which they are regularly called upon to do at parties. They generally practice these skills in private, a custom that is called *jang ki,* or "favorite technique."

Jimmu kyuchik (jeem-muu kyu-cheek)—"Company rules," something every company in Korea should have, and should require all new employees to sign as one of the conditions of employment.

Joja sei (joe-jah-say-e)—It has historically been dangerous for individual Koreans to stand out in a crowd or to draw attention to themselves when things go wrong or there is any kind of problem. Under these circumstances, it is common for them to *joja sei,* or "lay low." This can and often does cause additional problems in a company when keeping quiet compounds the situation.

Joong-in (joong-inn)—The *joong-in,* or upper-middle class, during Korea's long feudal period was made up mostly of professionals, including doctors, lawyers, translators, and middle-ranked military officers. The same groups are prominent in today's society, but are no longer hereditary or so clearly defined.

Junggi chaeyong (juung-ghee chay-yong)—This is "periodic hiring," and refers to the custom of Korean companies hiring high school and university graduates in batches in March, when the school year ends.

Jupan i anmaja (juu-pahn ee ahn-mah-jah)—When Koreans feel that a price is too high, they are likely to say *jupan i anmaja* or that their "abacus is unbalanced."

Jwachon (jwah-choan)—Literally a "change to the left," this term refers to someone being demoted or transferred to a job with less prestige. It comes from the old custom of seating inferiors on the left.

Kanpan (kahn-pahn)—This is the Korean equivalent of the famous Japanese word *kanban,* which originally meant "sign" or "bulletin board," but now refers to the "just-in-time" delivery system made famous by Japanese manufacturers. Korean companies have adapted the system to their own manufacturing process.

Keiyul hoesa (kay-e-yuul hay-sah)—Korean companies are generally "aligned" with one of the major *chaebol* groups, and are known as *keiyul hoesa,* or "affiliated companies." Which group a particular company belongs to can have a significant influence on its overall business, from its ability to raise capital to how effectively it can distribute and promote products in the Korean market. Foreign companies contemplating going into business with Korean firms should identify and familiarize themselves with their group affiliations.

Keo mul (kay-oh muul)—A man of exceptional power and influence is often referred to as a *keo mul,* or "big shot."

Kibu (kee-buu)—Surprisingly, one of the "problems" of doing business in Korea is the pressure brought on companies to make frequent and sizeable *kibu* (donations) for causes that range from the very worthwhile to the very obscure and doubtful. It is often advisable to investigate groups soliciting donations before parting with your money. Even legitimate organizations tend to overdo it, however.

Kibun (kee-buun)—This meaningful word refers to one's feelings, mood, or state of mind. Great care is taken by Koreans to avoid having their *kibun* lowered or hurt in any way. They are equally concerned about hurting the *kibun* of anyone else. This means that criticism and bad news are often withheld or substantially toned down, sometimes resulting in misinformation and later problems.

Kibun jokye (kee-buun joe-kay)—This refers to the "face" or "manner" that one presents to others to ensure that they will feel good, friendly, etc.

Kioe chae yong (kee-way chay yong)—"Hiring out-of-season," or the practice of hiring new employees at times other than following graduation, when most companies do their annual hiring.

Kisongpumui (kee-song-pume-we)—"Ready-made," as in clothing. Korean ready-made clothes were of sufficient quality by 1986 to have made major inroads into the Japanese market, the most demanding in the world.

Ko e kulmyun (koe ee kuul-me-uun), **Gui e kulmyun** (gwee ee kuul-me-uun) These two terms mean "nose ring" and "earring," and are used in reference to a situation or thing (such as a contract) that can be interpreted in two or more ways, or a person who changes his attitude or position to suit the circumstances.

Kolpu (kole-puu)—This is Korean for "golf," an activity that is seen by Korean businessmen as an important part of their internationalizing.

Komun (koe-muun)—A Korean *komun* (consultant or advisor), especially one of high social standing with important government and industry contacts, can be invaluable to foreign companies in Korea or those wanting to do business with Korea. Retired government officials from key ministries as well as company executives from leading firms are also much in demand for their knowledge and network of contacts.

Kongja (kong-jah)—This is the Korean word for Confucius, perhaps the most important figure in Korean history. Familiarity with the primary teachings of Confucius is a great asset in understanding the attitudes and customs of Koreans.

Kongjung-in (kong-jung-een)—Because of the need for so many official documents in Korea, the profession of *kongjung-in*, or "notary public," is popular.

Kongson (kong-soan)—Politeness (*kongson*), combined with Confucian-style respect, is one of the primary facets of the Korean social system. Koreans tend to be very formal in business and official relations. Generally speaking, businessmen, government officials, and other professionals in the company of foreigners relax completely only during nighttime drinking parties.

Korae (koe-rye)—Given the extraordinary compulsion Koreans have for bettering themselves, and the equally competitive nature of the economy, smaller independent businessmen are constantly on the lookout for *korae*, or business deals. Their enthusiasm is so great it frequently bypasses their ability to perform. Newcomers should be aware of this factor, and be sufficiently thorough in checking out potential business partners.

Kukche kyohon   (kook-chay k'yoe-hoan)—International marriages (*kukche kyohon*), particularly between American men and Korean women, have been fairly commonplace since the early 1950s, when the U.S. began stationing large numbers of troops and civilian workers there. Korean women have been renowned for ages for their beauty, strength, loyalty, and other sterling qualities—to the extent that they were once regarded as one of the reasons why neighboring nations were motivated to conquer Korea.

Kukpiui   (kook-pee-we)—With their family orientation, which extends to companies, Koreans do not think of such things as personal problems, financial affairs, and the like as matters to be treated as confidential (*kukpiui*). This cultural characteristic often upsets foreigners who are not accustomed to such things being openly discussed, particularly matters concerning wages, bonuses, and company business.

Kwalli   (kwahl-lee)—Korean social science professors and other scholarly types often say there is no such thing as Korean-style management (*kwalli*), then go on to describe a system that is typically Korean. What they apparently mean is that there is not one uniform style of management in Korea, but a number of "styles" that differ to varying degrees, being mixtures of Korean and Western approaches, along with features that reflect the individual philosophies and experiences of their founders or leaders.

Kyesanso   (kay-sahn-soe)—This is the kind of bill or check one gets in a restaurant, which frequently results in a tug-of-war or a flurry of arm wrestling with fellow Korean diners who will frequently try to take the bill by force and pay it. Many foreigners who are subjected to this physical assault give up the struggle fairly quickly, out of embarrassment, even when they know it is their place to pay.

Kyeyak   (kay-yahk)—Because of the personal nature of the business system in Korea, a *kyeyak*, or contract, may be regarded as a personal arrangement between the individuals who signed it. This makes it extremely important for foreign companies to establish and maintain close personal relations with all levels of management in Korean firms they deal with.

Kyojesul (kyoe-jay-suul)—This interesting word means "business drink," and is indicative of the importance of official and ceremonial drinking in Korea's world of business. Many occasions in business dealings and relationships have traditionally been marked by a round of ceremonial drinking.

Kyonbon (kyoan-bone)—Much to the surprise and dismay of foreign businessmen, Korean customs often charge duties on product samples (*kyonbon*). Customs officials have a considerable amount of personal discretion in whether or not duties are charged, and at what rate.

Kyongjaeng (kyong-jang)—Competition (*kyongjaeng*) is a way of life in Korea. There is intense rivalry for the best education, the best job, the best of everything. Competition is on an individual, family, group, or company, as well as a national basis. It is one of the reasons for the remarkable economic advances made by Korea since the 1960s.

Kyosop (k'yoe-sop)—Koreans are skilled at negotiation (*kyosop*), in part because theirs is a very emotional culture with a highly refined verbal etiquette that makes it necessary for everyone to develop the ability to speak effectively, to manipulate the feelings of others, and to win by persuasion.

Kyoyuk (k'yoe-yuke)—Koreans are compulsive about getting an education (*kyoyuk*) because it has traditionally been one of the principal criteria for determining social class and advancement. For much of their long feudal history, which actually did not end until 1945, only members of the hereditary upper class could aspire to a higher education and to positions of authority. Now that education is open to all, and access to the official power structure is still decided on the basis of education, Korean parents go to extreme lengths to see that their children get the best possible education, with the greatest achievement being several years of postgraduate study in the U.S.

Maeddugi hanchul   (may-duu-ghee hahn-chuul)—This refers to the seasons when retail outlets are the busiest and make the most profits. The term literally means "grasshopper season," from the fact that during the short harvest season in Korea grasshoppers eat with an intense frenzy, knowing that the food supply will disappear with the coming cold.

Mal i manta   (mahl ee mahn-tah)—"Many words" or "one who talks too much," used in reference to a person who attempts to use logic over feelings, or cold reason over personal considerations. In Korea, people who try to use logic all the time and do a lot of talking are generally regarded with disdain, since this goes against the grain of a society based on human and personal feelings.

Mansei   (mahn-say)—This is the Korean equivalent of the Japanese *banzai*, but its use is slightly different. In Korea it is most often used at sporting events when someone wins or does something spectacular. In business it is customarily used to celebrate the signing of a contract or the accomplishment of an especially difficult task. It is a shout expressing pleasure and joy on an auspicious occasion. The closest English equivalent is "Hip! Hip! Hooray!"

Mitopop   (meet-tah-pop)—This is Korean for the "metric system," which is standard in Korea.

Mogaji   (moe-gah-jee)—This is an old way of expressing the concept of dismissing or firing someone. It literally means to cut off one's head: *Mogaji taranada,* upon which the head flies away.

Mojo   (moe-joe)—Shoppers in Korea are often advised to be wary of imitation gems (*mojo posok*), but copies (*mobang*) of famous-brand products are more common than fake gems.

Mok   (mock)—Korean imports and exports are often controlled by government-dispensed quotas (*mok*) based on the previous year's performance. This system has allowed individual companies to monopolize some import and export categories.

Mulmul kyohwan (muul-muul kyoe-hwahn)—The more sophisticated forms of *mulmul kyohwan* (barter) practiced in the U.S., particularly reverse inversion brokering, are still rare in Korea, but there is growing interest.

Mumohan (muu-moe-hahn)—Koreans are noted for their hospitality, which often verges on the extreme and derives from a compelling urge to both please and impress. This behavior gives the impression that they are unreasonably *mumohan,* or "extravagant" by nature, often to their own detriment, but when others are conditioned to the same custom it all balances out.

Munan kanda (muun-ahn kahn-dah)—This is an institutionalized expression used to people of an equal or lower rank when inquiring about how things are going with them. It means "go and ask if someone is at peace" (because historically there were so many wars in Korea).

Munhwa (muun-whah)—Koreans are very proud of their *munhwa,* or culture, and this pride is an important part of their nationalism, their attitudes toward foreigners, and their treatment of foreign businessmen. Foreign visitors and residents in Korea are expected to exhibit suitable interest in the cultural accomplishments of the country, and to respect both cultural artifacts and laws that mandate a cultural component in many business decisions.

Myongham (m'yong-hahm)—The name-card, or *myongham,* is more important in Korea than in Japan (where you hardly exist if you don't have one) because so many Koreans have the same family name (over half of the population is named Lee, Pak, Choi, Kim, or Chung). It is important that one's title be clearly stated on the name-card in order to effectively identify the person.

Myungmul (me-yung-muul)—Each of the major geographical areas in Korea has a certain number of *myungmul,* or "famous products," for which it has been noted for centuries. The items are popular among Korean travelers from other areas as gifts and souvenirs.

Naekyu (nay-kyu)—"Unwritten rules." Government ministries and agencies in Korea are known for having numerous unwritten rules that may or may not be applied, and may also be applied in a different manner or to different degrees by different individuals. This is one of the reasons that it is so important for foreign businessmen to have the input and guidance of someone who has been on the scene for a long time and knows how to get around and through the maze of *naekyu*.

Nat dungjang (naht duung-jahng)—Literally "day lamp," this term is a derogatory reference to people in companies—often managers and executives—who do very little work and appear to make little or no contribution to their departments—much as lights left on during the day.

Noemul (noh-muul)—Bribes (*noemul*) are rare in Korea. There are often payoffs of one kind or another on high-level business and political deals, but the kind of low-level bribery that is institutionalized in some countries goes against the very grain of Korean attitudes and behavior.

Nollijogin (nole-lee-joag-een)—The Westerner in Korea automatically expects Koreans to react in a logical, or *nollijogin*, manner based on their own cultural experiences. However, this is generally not the case, since Koreans have been culturally conditioned for centuries to react on the basis of personal factors and prevailing circumstances, which may not only be inherently different but changeable. It is necessary to have some knowledge of Korean attitudes and typical behavior before you can predict their reaction to a given setting, since it may not be "logical" in the Western sense.

Noryon-ga (no-ree-own-gah)—Because of their long history of venerating scholarship and knowledge, Koreans have a great deal of respect for true experts (*noryon-ga*). This has proven to be a significant advantage to foreign professionals associated with Korean companies.

Nunch'i (nuun-chee)—This is sometimes translated as "face-reading," but it goes beyond that to something that verges on telepathy. It refers to the nonverbal cues given by Koreans in their daily intercourse with each other when they do not want to come right out and say something that might be controversial or cause the other person to lose face. They depend on the other party to read their *nunch'i* and divine their unspoken thoughts or intentions. Koreans often automatically assume that Westerners are also experienced at this subtle form of nonverbal communication, just as often with unhappy results.

Ockji (oak-jee)—A familiar word in the Korean business lexicon, *ockji* means "I'll do it anyway" when given a task that appears to be impossible.

Ondanghan (own-dahng-hahn)—The Korean concept of *ondanghan*, or "fair," often differs from the Western interpretation because it is not necessarily an absolute principle, and changes with circumstances. For example, Koreans believe it is unfair for the U.S. to expect reciprocal access to its market, which is much smaller and more vulnerable than the American market.

Ondol (own-dole)—Sometime before the first century B.C., Koreans developed a central radiant heating system to warm their homes and buildings during the cold winter months—more than two thousand years before central heating was to become common anywhere else in the world. The system consisted of running pipes beneath the floors of buildings and forcing the heat from wood-burning stoves to circulate through the pipes. People sat and slept on mats on the warm floors. The *ondol* system of heating is still common in Korea.

Oryo u shijiman (oh-ree-yoe uu she-jee-mahn)—Another institutional phrase that is used often in Korea, this means in essence, "I know it is difficult but please do your best (to do me a favor or help me get something done)."

Pangsongmang (pahng-song-mahng)—The nature of Korean society has resulted in the use of *pangsongmang*, or networks, as the primary form of mutual help and cooperation in both private matters and in business. The institutionalized networks include the extended family, school classmates, people born in the same village or town, friends made while serving in the military and while working for the same government agencies or ministries.

Piso (pee-soe)—Foreign managers working in Korea are advised to hire their own private secretaries (*piso*)—as opposed to allowing a joint-venture partner or someone else to hire them—in order to ensure a greater degree of loyalty and obligation.

Poikotu (poy-kot-tuu)—Becasue of national and cultural cohesiveness, Koreans are often able to act together for popular causes in a way that is the envy of such polycultural and -racial countries as the U.S. One instance of this is boycotts (*poikotu*) against the products of countries that offend them. On other occasions, said one Korean business executive, "We simply order our wives and family not to buy certain products."

Ponggonjogin (pong-gahn-joe-gheen)—Many of the social and political tenets of Korea are still basically *ponggonjogin* (feudal), and often interfere wtih the attempts of the Koreans to adopt a democratic form of government and society. Feudalistic thinking plays a significant role in the management of many government offices and companies.

Ponosu (poe-no-suu)—The twice-a-year bonus (*ponosu*) has become an integral part of the income of company employees in Korea. Companies are often called on to pay bonuses even when profits do not warrant them. This is done to avoid disappointing and angering employees as well as to maintain the firm's public reputation.

Pop (pap)—Korean law (*pop*) is said to be much more like German law than American law, and is therefore difficult for Americans to understand and appreciate. There is also a strong tendency to interpret the law from both a Confucian and nationalistic bias.

Posu (poe-suu)—It is often said that Koreans work for bosses (*posu*) instead of companies (the opposite of the Japanese), because of the deep personal bonds that are essential for Koreans to maintain a successful relationship, whether privately or in business. As a result of this, Korean workers often display more loyalty to their immediate bosses than to their employers.

Puha (puu-hah)—The role of the *puha,* or "follower," in Korean companies is of vital importance, especially when the chairman of the board or the president decides to step down. In most cases, company heads are regarded as "dynasties" in which the retiring leader has the right to name his successor, often his most faithful follower or the one whom he thinks is most likely to continue his philosophy and policies.

Puin (puu-een)—Another person's wife. Also, **ojumoni** (oh-juu-moe-nee).

Pumjil (pume-jeel)—With their long history as manufacturers of handicrafts which long ago achieved the *pumjil* (quality) of fine arts, Koreans have a cultural sense of and natural desire for both good design and quality in all of their products. These deeply entrenched traits were a major factor in their rapid emergence as an exporting nation.

Pummi (pume-mee)—This word refers to decision-making through the circulation of written documents (and is the equivalent of Japan's *ringi seido* or "document system"). Very few Korean companies use the *pummi* system in its pure form, although some Western businessmen operating in Korea find it useful because it at least provides documentation for what is going on in companies (where written memos and similar records are rare).

Pyonhosa (pyone-hoe-sah)—There are few *pyonhosa* (attorneys) in Korea because the Korean concept of personal and business relations generally precludes their use in settling disputes or negotiating business or financial deals. Korean executives who were educated abroad are, of course, much more comfortable with the use of attorneys in their business dealings.

Pyong (p'yong)—One *pyong* is a specific measurement of 3.3 square meters, and is used to describe the size of plots of land, the floor space of buildings, etc. The number of *pyong* in a person's home or apartment is a measure of one's social status.

Rotori (roe-tah-ree)—This is the Korean pronunciation of "rotary," which refers to a traffic circle. For some reason, there are many rotaries in Seoul, and until you get used to them they can make driving in the city more confusing than usual.

Sagwa (sahg-wah)—The *sagwa,* or apology, is an important part of interpersonal relations in Korea because of the
strong compulsion not to give offense to anyone for anything. Because of the strict system of etiquette, Koreans
find that frequent apologies on all kinds of occasions, including what may appear to be trifling concerns to outsiders, are the better part of valor.

Sang-min (sahng-meen)—The lower-middle class in feudal Korea (*sangmin*) was made up of artists, craftsmen,
fishermen, farmers, and merchants.

Sangpyo (sahng-pyoe)—Korean consumers are very
sangpyo, or brand-conscious. Those who can afford it often
prefer to buy famous international brands even when
equivalent Korean-made products are available.

Sasaenghwal (sah-sang-whal)—The concept of *sasaenghwal,* or privacy, is not nearly as explicit or as strong in
Korea as it is in much of the West. Because of the commu-
nal nature of life during their long feudal period, Koreans
could have few secrets from each other. When this was
combined with the Confucian concept of suppressing individuality in the interest of the group, a desire for personal
privacy was considered an aberration. The tendency for
Korean employees to be unconcerned about keeping
things private is often upsetting to foreign managers.

Seibei (say-bay)—At the beginning of the new business
year, usually between January 3 and 5, it is customary for
Korean businessmen to make courtesy calls on the directors and presidents of their client or customer companies
to bow and ask for their continued patronage during the
new year. This custom is known as *seibei,* or "beginning of
the year bow."

Seoncho haget sumnida (say-own-choe hah-gate sume-
nee-dah)—"I will take care of it." This commonly used
phrase, when translated into English, implies that whatever the problem or request, the individual making the
statement intends to literally take care of it—to come
through. In the original Korean, however, this meaning is
not so explicit. It means something more like "I will do my
best but I'm not making any promises"—which is a very

common cop-out when you have no intention of doing anything at all.

Sahun (sah-huun)—Virtually all larger Korean companies have their own *sahun*, or slogans and "company precepts." Most of the slogans and statements represent the personal philosophies of the founders. In some Korean companies, these precepts are read aloud at morning meetings and on special occasions.

Sapyo (sah-pee-yoe)—It is rare for Korean employees to leave a large, well-known company. When they do, most write *sapyo*, or formal resignation letters, stating their reasons. If the employee is considered valuable by top management, considerable effort may be made to persuade him to remain with the company.

Seiryuk kwon (say-ree-yuke kwahn)—Literally, "power place," this term refers to a favored bar or cabaret which one frequents often, is well known by the management and staff, and therefore has "influence." Businessmen like to take guests, especially foreign visitors, to their *seiryuk kwon* because they are assured of special service, and the guests are more likely to be impressed with the businessmen.

Shigan-ul omsuhanun (she-ghan-ule ohm-suu-hah-nuun)—Possibly because of the strict military training most Korean men undergo, they tend to be very punctual (*shigan-ul omsuhanun*), and expect the same of others.

Shihom (she-home)—*Shihom*, or "examinations," are a fact of life for young Koreans. Each educational step upward is marked by increasingly difficult examinations, with the most difficult being the one to enter a prestigious university. Finally, those seeking jobs with the more desirable commercial companies and government offices must also pass tough examinations that weed out all but the brightest.

Shijo (she-joe)—More so perhaps than in most countries, the *shijo* (founders) of Korean companies tend to mold them totally from top to bottom in the image of their own management as well as social philosophies. One of the first things one should find out about a Korean company is whether or not it is still headed by its founder, and if so, to obtain as deep an understanding as possible of his personal beliefs and policies.

Shikunbap (she-kuun-bahp)—"Cold food." When an individual in a company or a government office or agency is shunted off of the promotional ladder, an obvious sign that he is not going to reach the higher executive levels, he is sometimes described as being fed *shikunbap,* or cold food. Most such people lose much of their power or influence within the company, since everyone knows they are not going to advance in the managerial hierarchy. Foreign businessmen approaching Korean companies should try to make sure they have not been shuffled off onto a "cold-food eater."

Shimushik (she-muu-sheek)—On the first day of business after the New Year holidays, Korean companies generally hold *shimushik,* or "starting business ceremonies," to mark the beginning of a new year. Executives and managers make short speeches in a festive atmosphere.

Shinyong (sheen-yong)—Interpersonal as well as business relations in Korea are based more on personal trust (*shinyong*) than on any code of ethics or philosophy or body of law. It is therefore vital that foreign businessmen establish strong personal bonds with their Korean agents or partners.

Shimalseo (she-mahl-say-oh)—A *shimalseo* is a "letter of apology," often written following some kind of problem as an official expression of regret aimed at repairing damaged relations.

Soju (soe-juu)—A "mild" liquor made from rye, sweet potatoes, and sometimes other grains, *soju* was introduced into Korea from Mongolia in the fourteenth century. It is a clear drink, resembling vodka.

Song (song)—Korea is apparently unique in that there are only a few dozen family names (*song*) in the whole country. Because of the serious problem of distinguishing between so many people with the same last name, it is becoming more common for people to adopt *pyolmyong* (pyole-myong), or nicknames. It is also common now for the initials of the first and middle (generational) name to be used as an aid in identifying the hundreds of thousands of Lees, Kims, Pahs, and Chois. Chong-Chill Kim becomes C. C. Kim.

Songbyul hoe   (song-be-ule hay)—Such events as departing for overseas assignments are ceremoniously observed in Korean companies by *songbyul hoe,* or "farewell parties," at which there are speeches and numerous toasts. The parties serve to strengthen personal ties among the employees and reinforce their attachment to the company.

Songgum   (song-gume)—There are a variety of restrictions controlling the remittance of money (*songgum*) out of Korea. Generally speaking, the government prefers that no profits be exported from the country. It is therefore important that this facet of any joint venture be clearly approved in advance.

Songsaeng   (song-sang)—*Songsaeng,* or teachers, have traditionally been highly respected in Korea, where education was so important in society. The term is still one of respect, and is often applied to professionals outside of the teaching profession as a way of showing special respect. It is also sometimes used to butter up individuals for one purpose or another. The honorific *nim,* which is the equivalent of "mister," is often added to *songsaeng.*

Sonmul   (soan-muul)—*Sonmul,* or gifts, are an important part of developing and maintaining social and business relations in Korea. Foreign businessmen who are not familiar with this custom should get experienced local advice on what kind of gifts are appropriate for particular occasions.

Soryu   (soe-r'yuu)—There is a contradiction in the use of *soryu* (documents) in Korea that is often both bothersome and a detriment to business. Very few documents are created in the regular course of business. Most of the interaction between managers and personnel is verbal and few written records are kept. This often leads to misinterpretation and confusion that can be straightened out only by additional meetings. On the other hand, excessive documentation is typical of government offices, agencies, and ministries, and is a special burden on businessmen.

Suchul haltangje (suu-chuule hahl-tahng-jay)—This term means "export quota system," and is an important facet of Korea's export industry.

Sungshil (suung-sheel)—One of the most important words in the Korean businessman's vocabulary, *sungshil* means "sincerity" or "integrity." It is the quality employers look for in new employees, and in general is regarded as more important than technical knowledge or skill. This is also the quality Korean businessmen first look for in their foreign contacts. They feel that without this quality in a relationship, it is better not to do business with the individual or company concerned.

Sunsu chida (suun-suu chee-dah)—"First to draw" or "first to strike," in reference to springing some kind of surprise on your negotiating counterpart and winning a major point, or putting your business opponent in a position where he has no more room to maneuver.

Tabang (tah-bahng)—Literally "tea rooms," these ubiquitous shops (there are some 35,000 of them in the country, with a quarter of these in Seoul) originally served only tea, but have evolved into the Korean equivalent of the coffee shop and serve a wide variety of drinks and food, and come in several kinds—those catering to businessmen, to young dating couples, to the affluent "café-set," and to gourmet coffee lovers. One of the most popular shops specializing in a variety of coffees is *GaMu* (gah-muu) in the Myongdong district of downtown Seoul. One peculiarity of the *tabang* is an arrangement between their association and the bakery association that any shop selling coffee will not sell pie.

Taeguk (tay-gook)—This is the national flag of Korea. It consists of a circle made up of interlocking red and blue halves which represent the flow of the seasons, with the red or *yang* half representing the sun, and the light, positive, masculine, active aspect of the cosmos, and the blue or *ying* side of representing the moon, and the feminine, passive, cold, dark aspect of cosmic forces.

Taeriin (tie-reen)—An agency (*taeriin*) is the easiest form of business relationship to establish in Korea, but there are a number of restrictions on the activities of agents of foreign firms that must be carefully weighed before deciding on this form of representation.

Taesa (tie-sah)—The position of *taesa*, or ambassador, to Korea is an interesting assignment that is also delicate and often frustrating because of cultural factors, including the Korean obsession-like pursuit of national economic goals. A veteran foreign ambassador in Seoul can be a valuable source of insight and information to an incoming company.

Taewu (tay-wuu)—This is a word that may be used on a card to mean something like "high rank" or "senior rank" without specifying a department or position. It is primarily used to describe the kind of service given to VIPs and special guests. Visiting businessmen are often given this kind of treatment (and thereafter feel obligated to their hosts and inclined to be less demanding in their negotiations).

Tallyok (tahl-yoak)—There are two *tallyok* (calendars) used in Korea, the lunar calendar and the solar calendar. Holidays from both of the calendars are celebrated, so it is important for businessmen to be familiar with both.

Tamye (tom-yay)—The Korean social etiquette that requires all favors and debts to be paid is known as *tamye*, which literally means "answering." This etiquette includes expressing thanks when appropriate, bowing, etc.

Tangchal yok (tahng chahl yahk)—Literally "power of insight," this term is used to describe the visceral feeling by which Korean businessmen often make decisions—as opposed to using intellectual reasoning or logic. Because of the pervasive cultural conditioning Koreans undergo, they are also able to communicate to an extraordinary degree without using words, almost as if by telepathy. Foreign businessmen dealing with Koreans are often nonplussed by this system of decision-making and communicating, often wasting a lot of time in trying to use logic when the Korean side is seeking to develop personal rapport. Another interesting word that makes reference to the belly area is *baet-chang,* or "leather belly," which refers to a man who really has no assets but behaves as if he were rich.

Tangol   (tahn-gole)—"Sweet place." This is a bar where a businessman has developed a close relationship with the owner or manager and the hostesses, and is treated as a special customer. It is a place he takes new friends and clients, and where he goes when he needs to have attractive women fuss over him and make him feel good. Such bars are also called *tanga* (tahn-gah).

Tanshin buin   (tahn-sheen buu-een)—This term refers to employees who are transferred from their original place of employment to a branch, subsidiary, or affiliated company, often in a distant city or even foreign country, away from their families, forcing them to take care of themselves, like bachelors. The assignments are serious hardships for many older employees with families, but they are common because Korean companies systematically transfer personnel around throughout their organizations as part of their on-the-job training.

Todok   (toe-dock)—Korean critics say *todok* (morality) in Korea is based on social factors rather than philosophical principles, and sometimes results in confusion and frustration in international business.

Tojang   (toe-jahng)—This is the name-seal Koreans customarily use in lieu of signing their names on ordinary letters or documents. Seals that are used for stamping official documents must be registered with the local authorities, and are known as *ingan* (een-gahn).

Tomping   (tome-peeng)—This is "dumping," pronounced in Korean, in which the "d" sound and "t" sound are often interchangeable and indistinguishable. Koreans are perhaps more sensitive to charges of "dumping" (selling their goods in foreign markets at lower than production costs) than the Japanese because their overall export volume is much smaller and they regard such accusations as unfair, if not racially motivated.

Tongchal yuk   (tong-chal yahk)—"Keen insight," the quality top Korean businessmen look for in managers being considered for higher executive positions. The individual with this kind of insight is one who has a conspicuously high level of intuitive intelligence and can be expected to make the right decisions most of the time.

Uishin jonshin (we-sheen joan-sheen)—Literally "from my heart to your heart" or "heart to heart," this is a type and level of communicaiton that takes place nonverbally, and is a kind of cultural telepathy. Products of an intensely personal culture that homogenizes them, Koreans often know what the other person is thinking without the use of words. It is the type of communicating they are naturally familiar with, and they often run into difficulty in dealing with foreigners because they take it for granted that the foreigner is on the same wavelength and is "receiving" their messages.

Undaeng i (unn-dang ee)—The Korean word for rear end, *undaeng i* is used in a number of compounds to describe specific types of people, from those who are slow or lazy to those who are a bit strange.

Wiom (we-ohm)—Older Koreans who are traditional in their attitudes and behavior put great stock in *wiom* (dignity), and it is important for one to react properly toward them, meaning politely, with studied restraint and grace. This does not mean, of course, that one should compromise on ethics or principles in acknowledging this deeply entrenched social custom.

Yangban (yahng-bahn)—The upper class in feudal Korea, made up of scholar-bureaucrats (*munban*) and high-ranking military officers (*mulban*). Many Koreans and foreign residents say the *yangban* social system still prevails, and now consists of high government bureaucrats, ranking military officers, and newly rich businessmen.

Yeon (yay-own)—The strict Confucian-oriented society of Korea makes it imperative that personal relations be established between two people before they can engage in business or interact socially. *Yeon* is the word for this personal relationship, which is established through acceptable introductions and then a number of face-to-face meetings that involve eating and drinking together, getting to know each other's personal background, and establishing common interests, trust, and confidence in each other. Because the personal relationship must precede any business dealings, it requires an investment in time, effort, and money that the foreign businessman is likely to regard as wasteful and foolish. And many, despite knowing about the requirements of *yeon,* will often ignore them and proceed as if they were in the U.S., where such personal requirements are minimal.

Yeon jul   (yay-own juul)—"Connections," something Koreans cannot do without. Virtually all areas of work and private life depend on making and maintaining networks of close personal connections. The foreign businessman who wants to succeed in Korea must develop and nurture the same kind of networks.

Yeui pomjol   (yay-we pahm-jahl)—The precepts of Confucianism, in which the relationships between the sexes, the young and the old, and the different social classes are carefully and minutely prescribed, are still very strong in Korea, with the result that special attention should be given to appropriate *yeui pomjol,* or etiquette, in all personal and business relations. Generally speaking, Korean etiquette is based on respecting one's parents and elders, on obeying superiors, on avoiding comments or behavior that would hurt the other person's feelings or harm their "face," bowing at the right time and in the right manner, saying the right things at the right time, and following age-old customs in matters relating to life's main passages—coming of age, marriage, death, etc.

Yojung   (yoe-juung)—This is what foreigners generally call a *kisaeng house. Kisaeng* actually means "hostess." *Yojung* means "inn," which in turn employs *kisaeng* to entertain its guests. *Kisaeng* are the equivalent of Japanese *geisha*—although some of them today are more like cabaret hostesses.

Yongan saengsan-go   (yoan-ghan sang-sahn-go)—Expatriate businessmen in Korea say the typical Korean manager's approach to increasing *yongan saengsahn-go,* or annual production, is to work his employees harder and longer hours.

Yonhoe (yoan-hoe-eh)—Koreans are noted for their extravagant hospitality, especially when it comes to food. Dinners for foreign guests are almost always *yonhoe* (banquets), involving numerous courses, a great deal of drinking, and often entertainment of some kind.

Yuhaeng (yuu-hang)—Like their close Japanese neighbors, Koreans are very *yuhaeng* (fashion) conscious and concerned about being well dressed. This has helped fuel the development of a growing fashion industry.

Yuhan Hoesa (yuu-hahn hoe-eh-sah)—A limited liability company, in which fifty is the maximum number of stockholders.

Yuryuk ja (yuu-ree-yuke jah)—Literally, "a person with influence," meaning someone with sufficient power or clout to make things happen, especially in reference to matters concerning the government, or getting someone a job in a desirable government agency or company. Many companies owe much of their success to having a *yuryuk ja* on their side.

Guide to Korean Pronunciation

Pronunciation Guide to Vowels

A	**Ya**	**Ŏ**	**Yŏ**	**O**
Ah	Yah	Ah	Yah	Oh
Yo	**U**	**Yu**	**Ŭ**	**I**
Yoh	Uu	Yuu	Oo	Ee

Pronunciation Guide to Multiple Vowels

Ae	**Yae**	**E**	**Ye**	**Oe**
Aeh	Yaeh	Eh	Yeh	Oeh
Wa	**Wŏ**	**Wae**	**We**	**Wi**
Wah	Wah	Wae	Weh	Wee

Pronunciation Guide for Syllables

Ka	**Kya**	**Kŏ**	**Kyŏ**	**Ko**
Kah	Kyah	Kah	Kyah	Koh
Kyo	**Ku**	**Kyu**	**Kŭ**	**Ki**
Kyoh	Kuu	Kyuu	Kuu	Kee

Note that the third syllable in the top line (Ŏ) is pronounced more like an "a" than an "o". For example *oje* (yesterday) is pronounced *ay-jay*. *Odiso* (where) is pronounced *ah-dee-soe*. I have attempted to account for this factor in the phonetics following each word and sentence.

Na	**Nya**	**Nŏ**	**Nyŏ**	**No**
Nah	Nyah	Noo	Nyoe	No

Nyo	**Nu**	**Nyu**	**Nŭ**	**Ni**
Nyoh	Nuu	Nyuu	Nuu	Nee

Da	**Dya**	**Dŏ**	**Dyŏ**	**Do**
Dah	Dyah	Doe	Dyoe	Doe

Dyo	**Du**	**Dyu**	**Dŭ**	**Di**
Dyoe	Duu	Dyuu	Due	Dee

Ra	**Rya**	**Rŏ**	**Ryŏ**	**Ro**
Rah	Ryah	Roe	Ryoe	Roe

Ryo	**Ru**	**Ryu**	**Rŭ**	**Ri**
Ryoe	Ruu	Ryuu	Rue	Ree

Ma	**Mya**	**Mŏ**	**Myŏ**	**Mo**
Mah	Myah	Moe	Myoe	Moe

Myo	**Mu**	**Muu**	**Mŭ**	**Mi**
Myoe	Muu	Myuu	Mue	Me

Ba	**Bya**	**Bŏ**	**Byŏ**	**Bo**
Bah	Byah	Boe	Byoe	Boe

Byo	**Bu**	**Byu**	**Bŭ**	**Bi**
Byoe	Buu	Byuu	Bue	Bee

Sa	**Sya**	**Sŏ**	**Syŏ**	**So**
Sah	Syah	Soe	Syoe	Soe

Syo	**Su**	**Syu**	**Sŭ**	**Si**
Syoe	Suu	Syuu	Sue	She

A	**Ya**	**Ŏ**	**Yŏ**	**O**
Ah	Yah	Ohh	Yeh	Oh

Yo	**U**	**Yu**	**Ŭ**	**I**
Yoe	Yuu	Yuu	Uu	Ee

Ja	**Jya**	**Yŏ**	**Jyŏ**	**Jo**
Jah	Jyah	Joe	Jyoe	Joe

Jyo	**Ju**	**Jyu**	**Jŭ**	**Ji**
Jyoe	Juu	Juu	Juu	Jee

Cha Chah	**Chya** Chyah	**Chŏ** Choe	**Chyŏ** Chyoe	**Cho** Choe
Chyo Chyoe	**Chu** Chuu	**Chyu** Chyuu	**Chŭ** Chuu	**Chi** Che
Ka Kah	**Kya** Kyah	**Kŏ** Koe	**Kyŏ** Hyoe	**Ko** Koe
Kyo Kyoe	**Kuu** kuu	**Kyu** Kyuu	**Kŭ** Kuu	**Ki** Kee
Ta Tah	**Tya** Tyah	**Tŏ** Toe	**Tyŏ** Tyoe	**To** Toe
Tyo Tyoe	**Tu** Tuu	**Tyu** Tyuu	**Tŭ** Tue	**Ti** Tee
Pa Pah	**Pya** Pyah	**Po** Poe	**Pyŏ** Pyoe	**Po** Poe
Pyo Pyoe	**Pu** Puu	**Pyu** Pyuu	**Pŭ** Puu	**Pi** Pee
Ha Hah	**Hya** Hyah	**Hŏ** Hoe	**Hyŏ** Hyoe	**Ho** Hoe
Hyo Hyoe	**Hu** Huu	**Hyu** Hyuu	**Hŭ** Hue	**Hi** Hee